THE
UNSTOPPABLES

THE
UNSTOPPABLES

SUCCESS STRATEGIES from 12 Top Women Leaders
to **SUPERCHARGE** Your Career

---■---

Mary Jane Mapes

THE UNSTOPPABLES

ISBN 978–0–9841609-6-9
eBook ISBN 978-0-9841609-7-6

Library of Congress Cataloging-in-Publication Data
Mapes, Mary Jane.

The Unstoppables: Success Strategies from 12 Top Women Leaders to Supercharge Your Career

by Mary Jane Mapes
Published by The Aligned Leader Institute

FIRST EDITION

Library of Congress Control Number: 2016904319

Printed in the United States of America

This and other books by Mary Jane Mapes are available through The Aligned Leader Institute
800 East Milham, Suite 200
Portage, MI 49024
800-851-2270
Quantity discounts are available.

Cover Design and Graphics by Karen Matson
Interior Design by Andrea Stork

Dedication

This book is dedicated to Betty Lee Ongley, Michigan's first female mayor and only female mayor of the City of Portage, the place I call home. Betty lives to serve, and at age 90 is still actively contributing her time, energy, and expertise on numerous boards, including the American Red Cross, Southwest Michigan Land Conservancy, Kalamazoo Russian Cultural Association, and the Professional Executive Association of Kalamazoo.

Betty has been an honored recipient of the local YWCA's Woman of Achievement Award; in 2009 she was honored with the ATHENA Award.

Betty Lee Ongley epitomizes the servant leader. To Betty and so many women like her, I owe my profound gratitude for being a shining example of what leadership is all about.

CONTENTS

PART ONE
LEADER PROFILES

PART TWO
LEADERSHIP CORNERSTONES

PART THREE
GROUP DISCUSSION QUESTIONS

Introduction:

WHY I WROTE THIS BOOK

Shortly after the Wall Street bubble burst in the spring of 2009, millions of us helplessly witnessed our life savings and investments evaporate. Shock and fear gripped our nation as we faced a shaky, uncertain future with telltale signs that there was a *new normal* and things would never again be quite the same. Determined to safeguard my profession as a consultant and speaker in this not so brave new world, I flew to San Francisco for a conference promising strategies for creating new opportunities in my profession.

Having worked with corporate leaders and their teams for over two decades, I had solid credentials and substantive content for clients with the need, money, and authority to hire me. I was concerned whether these clients still existed, and I wanted new ways of securing my position in the industry. Alas, the conference provided far more hype than helpful or practical application. The trip would have felt like a total bust had it not been for a late night chat with a colleague that turned me in a new direction.

Our conversation had shifted from disappointment with this meeting to what we both wanted our lives to look like in the future. The two of us had not only invested many years working as volunteer leaders in business and professional associations, but most of our adult lives as consultants, facilitators, and trainers. We had consulted with leaders at every organizational level, both in the US and abroad.

We were both strong, independent women who had crafted successful career paths for ourselves in a male dominated, corporate world. Each of us felt comfortable and confident in our professional positions, and we had worked hard to get there. We both enthusiastically agreed that working with women leaders had resulted in some of our most enjoyable and fascinating learning experiences. What was it about women in leadership that we found so exciting?

While some of our accomplished executives had already shattered the glass ceiling, many of them had broken new ground in their respective fields, holding their own in high-level positions often still considered the stronghold of men in our society. We knew from experience that women who achieved uncommon levels of success often worked harder, served more, and accomplished more, while struggling and sacrificing more as well. Their leadership journeys were compelling, often heroic, representing stories of personal courage and perseverance as they forged a pathway for other women aspiring for greater responsibility.

As we discussed our similar experiences with "stand out" women leaders, I realized that there existed a wealth of untapped lessons and practices for women wanting to enhance their effectiveness as leaders regardless of the arena. It occurred to me that many women were not just *receptive* to lessons that could accelerate their growth, but were *seeking* them to provide roadmaps for their own journeys. And who better to teach these women leaders than those who had already made it to the highest levels of organizational leadership? Why not provide a first-hand account of what it took to reach the top? That was the moment this book began taking shape.

What if I could gather stories and lessons from some of the most successful women leaders I could find and share these accounts with women on a leadership path? It can be a lonely trip to the Board Room. Why travel alone? Why not offer a resource to help aspiring women shorten their learning curve, accrue practical knowledge through the voices of experience, and develop competencies and skills, while avoiding some common pitfalls and mistakes along the way?

I began creating a list of women who, though not universally known, had made it to the senior level of their organizations and had thrived in the process. I wanted women who understood both personal and position power, and the difference between the two. I looked for leaders who had been willing to grow, experience, and learn from failure on their way to something greater. I wanted women who were called to accept greater responsibility with grace instead of grandeur as they worked their way to the top. And I found them.

One of my leaders, Dr. Ruth Shaw, stated, *"The position is not about you; you won't fully realize that until you are president or CEO or in another senior position. One day you leave that job and the lights don't even flicker. You see, a lot goes with the position itself, and it is NOT about you. It's about authority, and the power and connections that position holds. Try to stay clear in your own mind about this. Nurture those things that are all about you and respect those things that go with the position."*

In my five years of interviewing the twelve powerful women leaders profiled in this book, I could clearly detect the personal power each developed through the decisions and choices she made at critical times in her life. Though each leader took a unique path, similarities between these women emerged: cultivating competency, connectivity, and strong character. Without exception, each leader placed a premium on communication and caring. All recognized the importance of building strong teams and solid relationships, making a personal commitment to the pursuit of excellence as she continually and passionately enhanced her capacity to lead effectively.

None of these women felt their jobs were easy. Far from it. Some of their biggest lessons were spawned from failure, and each woman had the confidence to learn from her mistakes and move on. It seemed that all twelve of these women leaders sought deeper knowledge from the unseen spiritual realm, and this became a powerful part of how she guided the course of her life and career success. All spoke about vision and values and universal truths that guided their personal and professional lives. They learned about developing strategic partnerships, working effectively with people, balancing work and home life, handling tough decisions and recovering from bad ones—all keys to maintaining a sense of inner calm in the eye of any storm they faced.

My hope is that you learn what *you* need from our unstoppable twelve leaders. I hope their stories will provide you with insight and inspiration to move forward toward your passion, whether you serve in a business or nonprofit environment, as a volunteer leader in your community, or in your home. May the words of wisdom in these personal accounts provide a shortcut to learning that will propel you toward new levels of responsibility and far greater contributions than you might ever have imagined. May the stories of these women and what they learned along their journey to the top tier of leadership inspire you to become unstoppable, too!

—Mary Jane Mapes

WHAT YOU SHOULD KNOW
BEFORE READING THIS BOOK

In preparation for writing this book, I interviewed more than twenty women in executive positions. All of them were exemplars of leadership and some were ground breakers in their respective fields. While I wish I could have profiled all twenty, I set a limit at twelve, choosing those who had reached high leadership levels against great odds.

In addition to my chosen twelve women leaders profiled in this book, you will read snippets about, and snatches from, many other achievers well worth featuring, some of whom I've known personally and who serve in my local community. As you read about the twelve (what I lovingly call) *Unstoppables*, note the importance they placed on investing in relationships and the important role those relationships played in helping these women reach the highest levels of their organizations. They chose their relationships wisely and nurtured them religiously, knowing that loyal followers, dependable colleagues, and steadfast stakeholders were critical to results. Yet, not one of these leaders forgot the importance of nurturing her family relationships. These high achieving women have poignant stories about how their personal relationships provided them with the support and encouragement needed, during both good and tough times, so they could sustain the commitment and energy essential for peak performance.

Part One introduces you to brief profiles of the twelve leaders I selected. Throughout the book you will learn more about each woman's essence, what drives her, what sustains her, and what motivates her to continually step into positions of increasing responsibility. You will also benefit from each leader's stories and sage advice about handling both adversity and success. But mostly you will find women who are strong, loving, competent, and wise—women who can help bolster your self-belief and confidence to quash the fear that stops many women from ever venturing forth toward their full leadership potential.

You will also appreciate the stories and voices of women not profiled or featured, but included in this book. They too have much to offer. From those who fight for social justice to the quiet "leader next door," you'll read about women who have worked hard, demonstrated courage and creativity, and made a difference in their own way. I have been personally inspired by every story, philosophy, and personal principle in this book. Based on what these leaders share in common in terms of values, vision, and practice, I was able to create a model of four essential components comprising not just effective, but exceptional leadership.

Part Two outlines The Four Cornerstones of Leadership: Character, Commitment, Core Work, and Contribution. Each cornerstone includes three elements presented in detail. Though certainly not all-inclusive, they do reflect the major themes derived from my interviews. In this section, these unstoppable leaders will speak to you, often in their own words; their voices are extraordinarily powerful and their stories are especially inspiring. You may also appreciate the additional stories and bits of advice from other women who have followed their passion to impressive levels of achievement.

Part Three urges corporate application—as a learning lab—whether approached as part of a corporate women's leadership study group or book club discussion. You will be asked to think deeply about your own experiences, both from the perspective of a leader and follower, and the lessons you've learned as a result. Such discussions provide insight and motivation for enhancing leadership development throughout the organization. Of course, strategies for application may differ depending on the organization and its culture.

Thoughts on Maximizing Your Reading Experience

To maximize your investment, I recommend that you purchase a journal (whatever style you prefer) to record your thoughts, insights, questions, and action items, whatever you wish to capture for future reference. You can use technology for this purpose, too, though literally writing down ideas with pen and paper is more intimate, involving a different part of your brain.

I encourage you to personalize this book; read it with pen or highlighter in hand; make notes in margins. Want to remember a quotation? Highlight it. Should you have a brainstorm as you read, write it down.

Make this book your personal property. Mark it up. Dog-ear pages for a quick retrieval of information or idea you really like.

Don't let an idea pass you by. Be committed to learning from the courageous women leaders who have gone before you; add their thoughts and suggestions to your own knowledge and understanding; and use this collective learning to chart a personal leadership path that is supercharged and perfect for you.

PART ONE

LEADER PROFILES

—— PROFILE ——

Lillian Bauder

MA, University of Michigan | PhD, University of Michigan

Leader at a Glance

Social activist turned *visionary* learner and leader whose unrelenting spirit, exceptional relationship building, and unwavering *character* beat the odds.

Career Synopsis

Lillian Bauder, a pioneer and leader in the academic, cultural, and corporate arenas, enjoyed a long and illustrious career spanning many decades. From a position as a professor to serving as dean at the University of Detroit, she moved on to become the transformational President and CEO of Cranbrook Educational Community.

During her 13-year tenure at Cranbrook, Lillian tackled major (and what she deemed), manageable, and resolvable problems. She then transferred to the corporate world, becoming Vice President for Corporate Affairs at Masco Corporation and Chairman and President of Masco Foundation. During her final five years at Masco, Lillian led corporate strategy, as well.

Honors and Achievements

In April 2014, she was honored with Cranbrook's prestigious *Founders Award*. Now retired, Lillian remained active as director or trustee of numerous community and professional organizations in Michigan, including the Skillman Foundation and DTE Energy (presiding director) until

Spring, 2015. Now living in Maryland, she continues to be asked to serve on boards, consult, deliver presentations, and teach.

The Interview

Meeting Lillian in person is an experience in itself. A tall, stately woman with a dancer's bearing, she warmly welcomed me into her home, leading me to the dining area and treating me to a cup of coffee. I was then gifted with an inspiring portrayal of a woman possessing extraordinary wisdom, intelligence, and political savvy.

Confiding that she was a rather private person, Lillian conceded that it seemed the right time to tell her story. Everything about this proud yet humble, elegant woman told me that I was in the presence of someone "a cut above." Her manner was reserved but approachable. Lillian appeared to be a serious-minded person, deeply committed to her professional responsibilities and the people who worked with her, or for her. I could tell that she considered every detail, missed nothing, and analyzed everything.

As the interview unfolded, I became acutely aware of this woman's soaring intellect. Highly disciplined, goal oriented, and socially conscious, Lillian, from an early age, championed causes for civil justice, including involvement in the Civil Rights Movement of the 1960s. Not only was she driven by a passion for her work, Lillian had an abiding concern for those whose lives would be affected by her decisions. She did not take this responsibility lightly. By the end of our interview, I felt respect and awe for this remarkable woman whose influence was felt not only in her career but her community as well.

Lillian Bauder evolved into a skilled strategist, relationship builder, and trusted counselor, stepping up to leadership from an early age. Because she gravitated toward solving complex problems, asking targeted questions others shied away from, and making tough statements where many would demur, people singled her out and sought her input.

Lillian's bold and decisive nature steered her into leadership positions where she made her mark as an influencer and contributor in each of the organizations she led. In hearing her story, what stood out for me were the enduring relationships she built and sustained; how she meticulously crafted her leadership team and worked with key people to accomplish her organizational objectives.

Pivotal Career Points

While her long list of achievements could fill a book, three specific incidents stand out as a mark of this woman's character. When Lillian became CEO of Cranbrook, the institution was dealing with complex financial issues. But with the help of two key trustees, F. Alan Smith (then CFO at General Motors), and Bob Vlasic, CEO of Vlasic Pickles and Vlasic Foods, Lillian brought in a transformational endowment of $48 million to the financially challenged institution.

Lillian enjoyed *"extraordinarily good relationships"* at Cranbrook. One of those relationships was with the AFSCME Union, known as a tough and stalwart organization. Meeting with union members twice a year in the Art Academy Auditorium, Lillian admits to engaging often in *"tense discussions, lightened by humor"* with the union. These discussions were private. In spite of the prior history of conflicting management-union relationships at Cranbrook, they worked out a new relationship, supported each other publicly, and accomplished a good deal during Lillian's tenure.

It was obvious that there existed a love-love relationship between Lillian and AFSCME. This was proven time and again by the fact that union members would go above and beyond for her. A worker might have an assignment to merely repair a light switch but would end up looking around for what else might need to be done in Lillian's work area, a gesture that goes beyond everyday practices.

Lillian told me that when she left Cranbrook, *"The union held a picnic for me, giving me an AFSCME T-shirt and flowers. Some members who had worked their way up the hierarchy requested that I receive a Steward's Badge, explaining that every union needs a great Steward, and that's what I had been for Cranbrook."*

This relationship proved extremely valuable in later years when Lillian and Richard Manoogian, CEO of Masco Corporation, were dealing with some very complex issues at the Detroit Institute of Arts. They needed the support of all the city council members in Detroit, plus the AFSCME union for some critical steps they needed to take. Because of her proven, trusted relationship with the union from her days at Cranbrook, AFSCME proffered the support that was needed to accomplish her goal.

While at Masco Corporation, true to her nature, Lillian played the role she had honed in the academic and cultural arenas, which was "trusted counselor," providing a channel for information flow. Thanks to Lillian's exceptional listening skills and honoring of confidences, people at every corporate level regarded her as someone they could talk to and trust.

Her discretion and dependable leadership made it possible for various areas to communicate more openly and effectively with each other and move forward as a whole. Whether working the corporate or the not-for-profit world, Lillian always had a firm grasp of what it takes to build and maintain solid relationships at a personal and organizational level.

Principles and Philosophy

If you were to ask, as I did, how Lillian Bauder would describe her personal philosophy underlying her accomplishments, she would tell you the following:

"Leadership is a major responsibility in that people must trust you. When you are a CEO, you carry this responsibility with you, night and day, or at least you should. You know that there are a whole lot of lives dependent on you and your final decisions. It is not that you don't include others in the thought processes, but the final decisions are yours. You are responsible for your decisions, and they affect the lives of many individuals, many families, and many organizations or institutions.

I think a person in a leadership position has to be politically astute. Initially, people are not necessarily astute when they move into leadership roles. But you have to become politically astute; you have to understand that not everyone wants you to succeed. You may get most people on your side, but not everybody will want to support you.

Consequently, you need to understand how to build a broad base of support; how to talk to people who oppose you and how to handle that one person on your board who always needs to meet privately with you before a big meeting, or who will publicly disagree with you. What was effective for me was to hold a private meeting with this person ahead of time so I could find out his or her concerns and resolve them privately. Political astuteness is absolutely critical in every effective leader."

Suggestion for Your Leadership Development

When I asked Lillian Bauder what advice she has for emerging leaders, here is what she said:

"Do not see life through a simple prism of one's sex, race, age, religion, ethnicity, or sexual orientation. Life is far more complex. I have had this conversation repeatedly with women who might be inclined to think that things happen because they are female or of a particular ethnicity. The truth is that life is more complex. If I had thought that every difficulty I encountered was because I am a woman, I never would have continued to succeed. This is a life lesson I've often shared and, as a result, I've been able to help younger career-minded women get beyond this mindset.

When I was younger, the assumption was that women could do everything. Many women become exhausted and burned out because they try to 'do it all' all of the time. Women need to understand that there are different ways in which we play out different stages in life. My biggest leadership mistake, which I think a lot of 'first women' fell into, is that I lost my work-life balance for a time, but only for a time. I was fortunate. Some women lose it for good."

CLOSING THOUGHTS

L illian believes that women *can* do it all, but for most women, it happens in stages, spanning decades of dedicated learning, experimenting, and growing. This is an important point to understand and internalize. Lillian emphasizes that this particularly pertains to younger women still raising their children who are struggling with how they will handle "doing and being everything" at home and work.

From my perspective, Lillian's comments about women trying to do all and be it all, all at once, struck home. For those of us trying to combine family and career, striking a balance between the two is critical. I was reminded of a book published in the mid-1980s titled *The Superwoman Syndrome*.

The idea that a woman *can* have it all, be it all, and do it all still exists. Granted, a small number of women seem to achieve that lofty goal, but at what price. For the rest of us (as Lillian Bauder so wisely states), patience, vision, and "sequencing"—mastering the ability to pace one's life path—can help a woman achieve the leadership positions she desires.

Maintaining a long-term career plan while focusing on making meaningful contributions at work *and* home transforms time into more of an asset than a liability. Even in retirement, Lillian continues contributing to society in ways that are meaningful to her. This speaks to the fact that leadership isn't a title or formal position; it's an inner drive that must be expressed. It's one that is unstoppable and impossible to quell—a drive fueled by a desire for excellence.

Aristotle put it best, *"We are what we repeatedly do. Excellence, then, is not an act, but a habit."* Lillian Bauder has made it a lifetime habit to seek excellence and settle for nothing less.

23

PROFILE

Patricia Caruso

BA, Lake Superior State University | MA, University of Michigan

Leader at a Glance

Compassionate leader and breakthrough prison reformer who aligned her *vision* and humanitarian *values* to revamp state prison systems and create a national corrections reentry initiative model.

Career Synopsis

Patricia Caruso's career began as a county controller, but her path took an unexpected turn into the field of Corrections where she remained for over two decades. Patricia's leadership journey in state corrections began when she was asked to take over as warden of a huge, multi-level state prison with a troubled history. This appointment was controversial. The director of corrections wanted a leader with integrity, someone who wasn't beholding to anyone in the system, and one who would ask tough questions and stay the course. Only the third person in the department's history that rose from the business side to warden level, Patricia served in this position for nine years.

She went on to serve as Regional Prison Administrator for two years. After working as the Deputy Director for some months, in July 2003 Patricia was appointed Director of the Michigan Department of Corrections. Under her leadership, the state's prison population and rate of recidivism dropped significantly.

Honors and Achievements

Advancing from assistant business manager to prison business manager to warden, Patricia Caruso was the first female to serve as Director of Michigan's Department of Corrections. Nationally, Patricia served as President of the North American Association of Wardens and Superintendents, Vice President of the American Correctional Association and President of the Association of State Correctional Administrators.

Patricia Caruso's prisoner reentry program focused on better preparing prisoners to return to productive, law abiding lives. It is considered a gold standard model and has been implemented by other correctional systems throughout the United States, resulting in reduced prison populations and lower recidivism rates.

Patricia earned a reputation for being fair and considerate in a tough-minded, discipline-oriented culture where caring is often considered a weakness or dangerous. But during her nine-year tenure as prison warden and eight years as the director of the state corrections department, she gained and maintained the loyalty of employees, even in the midst of prison closings and job losses.

She also worked with the National Institute of Corrections to develop a women's leadership program for the Michigan Department of Corrections. In 2012, she was inducted into the Michigan Women's Hall of Fame.

The Interview

I was greeted with a disarming smile as I exited the elevator just outside Patricia Caruso's office. On first impression, I sensed her warmth and friendliness without fully capturing the depth and breadth of her strength and conviction.

Considering the prison backdrop, perhaps I expected a tall, commanding woman with a "take charge" exterior. But it didn't take long to realize I was in the presence of a dynamic personality in this small package. Animated and energetic, Patricia speaks with confidence, spirit, and a sparkle in her eye. I was captivated by her story as she shared her experiences and lessons learned as a woman leader in an undeniably tough profession. Fully committed to a vision for her department, she communicated with passion about what she and her colleagues were able to accomplish.

If you met Patricia, you would instantly detect that she's a "people person" who is genuinely concerned about the welfare and well-being of those for whom she is responsible, with a set of steely nerves that fortify and drive her vision.

Patricia's story embodies not just an aligned leader, willing to stand up for her strongly held beliefs and values, but someone who successfully influences others. Guided by an unbeatable combination of "head and heart," her accomplishments speak for themselves. Her driving passion to do the right thing allowed her to significantly alter a system affecting a population most of us seldom empathize with or understand—prisoners and parolees.

With a propensity to question the status quo, it was against Patricia's nature to simply accept existing rules or practices. She examined the entirety of a situation to grasp not just the process but also the implications of potential outcomes before taking action. Combining her natural curiosity with innate fearlessness, Patricia was never afraid to ask, *"Why do we do that?"* or to say, *"That doesn't make sense."* Being told, *"Because we've always done it this way,"* was never an acceptable answer. Patricia sought innovative solutions that stretched far beyond current practices and perceptions of the corrections world.

As Director of the Michigan Department of Corrections, Patricia was responsible for 18,000 employees, 44,000 inmates in 34 prison facilities, and upwards of 80,000 parolees and probationers throughout the state. She was able to communicate and "sell" her story to diverse audiences from staff and prisoners to community members, all the way to legislators and the governor's office.

Patricia kept her staff well informed and focused on the importance of doing the right thing because it was the only thing to do. She communicated the vision and mission often, reinforcing the part each person played in making it happen. She stressed the significance of personal accountability and the value of building quality relationships. When mistakes were made, she focused attention on what could be learned from them, and how important it was to maintain a positive attitude. This and more is what it took to influence an institutional culture not given to sweeping changes.

Pivotal Career Points

During her entire tenure, with the economy stuck in a downturn, the state budget was in desperate shape. Her uncanny ability to educate, encourage, and instill hope in the face of economic adversity inspired her staff to believe there was a "better way" and work toward it. In a time of slashed budgets, Patricia succeeded in trimming the cost of prison operations by significantly reducing the prison population and its recidivism rate.

As with other leaders featured in this book, Patricia Caruso's contributions were significant and long-lived. Most notable was reducing the recidivism rate through increased local support. Patricia shared her vision of safer communities with stakeholders, getting them actively involved in the prisoner reentry process. This groundbreaking model continues to draw national attention and recognition.

In Patricia's view, her responsibilities as corrections director were twofold: keep the community safe by incarcerating criminals and by rehabilitating prisoners so that, when released, they could rejoin society and function in the community as responsible, law-abiding citizens. This approach was markedly different from the traditional practice of keeping offenders incarcerated as long as possible.

Patricia demonstrated her unwavering character by taking and maintaining a remarkably courageous stance during one of her most challenging times as director. A parolee committed a series of horrible murders that made the headlines every day for six weeks. Patricia's staff felt defeated because everyone seemed to be desperately looking for someone to blame.

A classic "witch hunt" approach of finding a scapegoat so the department, its director, or the governor could appear free of any wrongdoing ran counter to Patricia's value of holding people accountable. In the face of accusations, effrontery, and turmoil, she kept employees focused on doing the right thing. It was a taxing effort, braving the forces of social outrage as people pointed fingers, wrote letters to the editor, and demanded that certain people be fired. The backlash was draining and demoralizing to her staff.

Patricia suffered many sleepless nights, knowing she might be just one phone call away from the next horrific headline. She constantly reminded the staff that they were running a big prison system, supervising parolees within communities throughout the state, and that bad things can, and do, happen. She reiterated that while risk cannot always be prevented or eliminated, the job of corrections was to *manage* the risk, which is why making the right decisions with scrupulous follow through was so critical.

Principles and Philosophy

Given the scope of her legacy, it was a pleasure asking Patricia to share her leadership philosophy. Her conviction and passion were evident as she spoke in her usual forthright manner:

"You have to be the kind of leader who is approachable because you need people around you who can say, 'The emperor wears no clothes.' If you surround yourself with 'yes people,' you are in deep trouble. You have to be someone people trust enough to say, 'I need to tell you that I think you're going down the wrong road on this.' If you don't have people who are comfortable enough to tell you that, you are left totally unprotected.

You need people who are willing to speak openly, and you need to be capable of hearing what they say, or you won't survive. Because the field of corrections is such a complex business with so many options and directions, you have to be able to hold robust discussions. We had many of those. And then collectively, we worked toward where we were headed.

For me, stress comes from the things you feel you cannot control. Even if the control you have is to walk away. There are certain things I have said over the years that I will not do. And I mean that absolutely; I won't do it. For me, this is a freeing feeling because I don't have to worry about making a decision I consider morally wrong or not right for my employees."

Suggestion for Your Leadership Development

Here is some solid, heartfelt advice on being a strong leader, from one small woman whose determination and commitment to service made a huge difference in her profession:

"It is very important to broaden your horizons. You cannot just stick with what you know or what history has told you. Transitioning from county government to corrections was a huge stretch for me, and I'm grateful to have had that opportunity.

I belong to a number of professional organizations because it's important to know what is going on in the world of corrections and those who interact with corrections. As a result, I have significantly changed my beliefs and approach to how we incarcerate offenders in this country. Initiating these changes is one of the reasons we have been able to reduce our prison population in Michigan.

I always encourage people to reach out and be involved in other organizations, even if, as in my case, your employer offers no financial support for your memberships. If you are not willing to do anything for yourself, outside of what your employer pays you for, you will never grow and flourish. You have to be willing to invest in yourself.

As a proponent of maintaining a positive attitude, I will admit that it's tempting to take offense and make yourself a victim or martyr. If you look to be offended, you will be offended every day, and so you have to take control of yourself, your career, and your life, and make that your decision. Own it. Sometimes we get all caught up in the transgressions, thinking, 'Everyone is picking on me,' or 'I don't have this opportunity.' If you look for these things, you'll find them. But don't make that who you are or you will be defined by that, and that is all you will ever be.

Decide that you will look at things positively and work from your strengths. Sometimes women get caught up in thinking, 'They won't let me do that because I am a female.' But that is seldom the reason why someone won't let you do something. Don't hold yourself back with this kind of thinking.

I often speak to women's groups about the issue of having it all, and the possible price of doing so. Keep in mind that you may not be able to have everything at the same time. Before being appointed state director, I was offered the deputy director position. I turned it down because I didn't want to pay the price. My daughter was 16 years old and a junior in high school, and taking that job would have meant living too far away from our home in Sault St. Marie. I didn't want to be a live-away-from-home mom.

It is critical to decide what your priorities are, and honor them. I made a decision to have children, I wanted to be a good parent, and I didn't want to put my personal needs ahead of theirs. I found a way to have a very challenging career while not feeling like I was sacrificing what I valued most, my family."

CLOSING THOUGHTS

Now retired from the Michigan Department of Corrections, Patricia continues her work as a much sought after consultant and speaker on the subject of prison reform. Considering the corrections culture, I can only imagine how many critics and skeptics stood on the sidelines when this seemingly unlikely woman took on an awesome responsibility that many leaders (male or female) would have run from.

She stands as an example of the adage, *"You never know what you can do until you try."* This stalwart woman didn't just try. She did it. She made it happen. So can you. I hope you will keep Patricia Caruso in mind when you face a career challenge that appears daunting. I am confident she'd tell you, *"If I could do it, you can, too!"*

PROFILE

Beth Jones

B.A., Boston University
Post-graduate Bible training and ordination,
RHEMA Bible Training Center, Tulsa, Oklahoma

Leader at a Glance

A woman who *forged ahead with fortitude*, inspired by her drive to meet the spiritual needs of people around the world through the spoken and written word.

Career Synopsis

Beth Jones, Senior Co-Pastor of Valley Family Church in Kalamazoo, Michigan, originally planned on becoming a dentist. But as a 19-year-old freshman, an unexpected spiritual transformation redirected her life into full-time ministry. After meeting and marrying her husband, Jeff Jones, in 1986, they were called to pioneer Valley Family Church in 1991, now with over 4000 members, making it one of the fastest growing Christian churches in the United States.

Honors and Achievements

Beth has authored over twenty books, including her *Getting a Grip on the Basics* series, which has been translated into several foreign languages. This popular series is enthusiastically used by thousands of churches in North America and around the world. It is no small feat to write an impressive series of books, and Beth stands as an example of the difference a truly inspired leader can make. Her ability to co-create, foster, and grow the church she and Jeff envisioned, from holding services in their home for a handful of people, to today's congregation of over 4000 members, the growth of Valley Family Church is no less than phenomenal.

The Interview

In meeting Beth Jones, she might initially strike you as serious, focused, and perhaps somewhat reserved, though she talks passionately about her work and her calling. If you dug deeper into her life and journey, you would be struck by how driven and fervent she is about her beliefs, how deeply engaged and creative she is in delivering her message, and how methodically she goes about implementing her action plans. Beth's approach to worship is simple; she wants people to "get it," and apparently, they do. The growth history of Valley Family Church stands as a silent testimony to what she and Jeff bring to the congregation on a daily basis.

"Consistent goodness and persistent pursuit" is the phrase that comes to mind as I listened to Beth describing her development as a woman leader in the church, her experiences along the way, and what she holds most important. From the podium, when filled with the Spirit, Beth is effusive and effervescent as she conveys her message to the congregation. In conversing one-on-one, she comes across as friendly, yet focused and strategic. What is consistent about her, though, is the compassion and love that shine in her eyes when speaking about her ministry.

After meeting and talking with Beth, it is easy to trace the roots of Valley Family Church from conception to reality, and how she and Jeff achieved their mission and vision. Of course, every church has its own atmosphere and ambiance, its own cadence and vibrancy, and its own way of delivering the message. Thanks to Beth and Jeff Jones, the Valley Family Church is a cut above. The moment you enter the premises, you are struck by the imaginative, loving attention to detail that went into making this place of worship one of the fastest growing churches in the U.S.

The modern interiors and thoughtful, creative features are both tasteful and practical. The stroller "parking area" is one example of a welcoming touch where the needs of families take precedence. Comfortable seating alcoves with closed circuit TVs for viewing the service from the atrium were created for the convenience of those who wish a different experience than that provided in the main sanctuary.

From the subtle security measures to the finishing touches to the stadium-style worship venue complete with amplifiers, you would be struck, as I was, by the devotion and detailed efforts that make you feel welcomed, loved, and cared for. Valley Family Church is a stunning place for fellowship and worship and a fitting tribute to the two pastors who conceived it.

Pivotal Career Points

Beth Jones broke tradition in the faith-based world. Young and eager, she stepped up to her calling of senior leader in a church that held a strong bias against women serving in such roles. Believing that she had been called to break through the "stained-glass ceiling," she took the initiative. Fully supported by her husband who held the door open for her to lead and speak, she blazed the way for other women of faith who felt called to senior positions.

In the early days, despite strong resistance and heavy criticism, Beth chose to dismiss rather than discuss traditional theological arguments about her role. It was her intent to rise above disagreement or dispute so she could do God's work in her unique way. Putting her faith in what she believed God was calling her to do, Beth was determined to let the fruit speak for itself.

Not too surprisingly, she prevailed over the detractors and critics. Her biggest challenge was in facing her internal adversaries—self-doubt and insecurity. But in receiving what she believed was a direct message from God (who spoke to her heart in quite bold terms), Beth held onto His words. *"I have called you to be a leader. Deal with it."* Much the same as an inspiring coach might speak to a gifted player, Beth took the message to heart, setting her focus on her mission and vision, moving forward and never looking back.

Principles and Philosophy

You may appreciate how Beth Jones defines her philosophy about leadership, while witnessing what she has accomplished, and why. Here is what she explained to me:

"Once we identify an individual or a group of people who are potential leaders, we like to put the ball in their court and say, 'Here is what we are looking for in our leaders and here is a process, a system, or the steps you can take to get to the next level of leadership.' Having a process in place is much better than just trying to convince people or assuming they want to be a leader. This growth and leadership process has worked very well for us by encouraging people to take steps that allow their gift to be evident and make a way.

Then, depending on the gifts and desires people have, and the various needs we have at the church, over time, people's talents will become evident, and they'll find their appropriate spot on the leadership team. It is really important to have a process in place, not only so that people can qualify themselves, but also so that we can identify potential leaders, as opposed to just guessing. This system gives people a chance to strategically demonstrate their gifts.

These types of processes, as well as other methods of recruiting, are crucial in the church world because we are highly volunteer-based, as opposed to having a massive budget to hire staff. The process is important because leaders like a challenge and want the bar set high. If you set the bar too low, you're not really going to attract real leaders.

One of the biggest challenges I have faced as a leader is carving out time to think, pray, plan, innovate, envision, and stay ahead of the overall organizational curve. In order to do this, I make it a point to maximize thinking time as well as being intentional about reading, gleaning information, and asking questions. In my particular role as a leader, I have to stay fresh, creatively and spiritually. The number one thing that keeps me motivated and keeps me honing my skills is my relationship with the Lord. I like to spend a lot of time with the book of Proverbs in the Bible because it is a book dedicated to wisdom. I also make a strong effort to spend time in prayer, seeking the Lord because He is the greatest leader, and I need His guidance. I also like to learn from others who have successfully blazed the leadership trail and are further down the road doing church the way we want to do it.

In addition to leading and ministering to our congregation each week, we endeavor to lead our dedicated staff in church-wide efforts to give back to our community through a variety of initiatives that help those in need. Personally, my husband and I are coming into a new season of leadership and are looking at how we can give back to empower other leaders in different ways. Through mentoring pastors, upcoming leaders, and this younger generation who sense God's call to the ministry, we are trying to leverage our experience, mistakes, and successes to coach others so they can go further in ministry, faster than we did!"

Suggestions for Your Leadership Development

Here are some words of wisdom from Beth Jones that range from the practical to the visionary. While the focus is on her faith and ministry, her ideas are applicable to any career endeavor.

"I tell young girls who aspire to leadership, 'Don't do what I did, which was being a reluctant leader and intentionally throwing "gutter balls" to prevent me from excelling or overachieving. That wasn't a good choice. If God has given you gifts and has called you to be a leader, be wise and go for it! You don't need to be a man; you don't need to wear the pants, you just need to be yourself, use your gifts, and let the fruit speak for itself. You can be both a very feminine woman, a really strong woman, and still utilize the gifts God has given you.'

I encourage all women to go for it—and then deliver. Don't be a woman who wants to be in leadership, and then once you're in the role, fail to deliver. It is simply one of the expectations of being in leadership; you are going to have to deliver once you get there. The bar is still set high for women in leadership, and that is not necessarily a bad thing.

To women in leadership I would say, 'This is your time! These days, if you are a young woman coming up, many trails have been blazed for you in every sector. The sky is the limit if you follow the Lord in His purpose and His plans for you. Don't throw gutter balls. Have a humble heart and a sweet spirit. Follow the Lord, and then have confidence to stand in whatever place of leadership He may want you to fulfill. There are divine callings on people to have great influence, women included, to do good things for people and great things for the Lord. Go for it. This is our time. Remember, promotion comes from the Lord, and you will reap what you sow, so go for it!'"

CLOSING THOUGHTS

Regardless of whether you aspire to serve in a church or secular arena, I hope that you will be inspired by Beth, the oldest sister of four girls, who came from a broken home. Raised by a single mother, Beth learned early on the importance of persevering in the face of tribulation, not allowing negative circumstances to define her. As someone once said, your beliefs determine your actions and your actions determine your results, but first you have to believe. With a strong belief in God, Beth Jones used her life struggles as a means of gaining a deeper understanding of herself, building a strong character, and discovering the hope required to fulfill on her life purpose.

Beth Jones is a groundbreaker, and I am confident that she would be the first to say, *"If my influence can extend beyond all that I ever thought or imagined I could do, with deep faith, yours can too!"*

PROFILE

Gail J. McGovern

BA, Johns Hopkins University
MBA, Columbia University

Leader at a Glance

Risk taker, course corrector, and innovative thinker who *fortified her foundation* and accepted Mission Impossible, steering a hopeless job toward the trajectory of a meteoric career.

Career Synopsis

Gail McGovern, leader in both the corporate and non-profit sectors, began her career at AT&T as a computer programmer, quickly moving up through sales, marketing, and general management assignments. She served as chief strategist of AT&T's communication services group and executive vice president of the $25 billion business markets division.

After leaving AT&T in 1998, Gail became President of Distribution and Devices for Fidelity Investments. Four years later, she took a faculty position at Harvard Business School, and in 2008 was recruited for the position of President and CEO of the American Red Cross. This line of work was the perfect fit, given her experience, leadership skills, and lifetime love of volunteering, a value deeply rooted in her upbringing.

Honors and Achievements

Besides serving at the helm of the American Red Cross, Gail is a member of the Board of Trustees of Johns Hopkins University and the Board of Directors of DTE Energy. In both 2000 and 2001, she was recognized by Fortune Magazine as one of the Top 50 Most Powerful Women in Corporate America.

Under Gail McGovern's direction, the Red Cross has become more effective in fulfilling its mission of emergency response and blood services, making it better prepared to face current and future challenges. Her transformational initiatives have led to improved financial stability while expanding the scope of lifesaving Red Cross services. She has initiated extensive modernization projects, including an overhaul of IT systems, enhancing the Red Cross's social media and mobile technologies with a series of free apps that put lifesaving skills at people's fingertips during emergencies.

During her tenure, McGovern has overseen the American Red Cross response to multiple high-profile disasters across the country and around the world, including the Haiti earthquake in 2010, the Japan earthquake and tsunami in 2011, Hurricane Sandy in 2012, plus a multitude of tornadoes, hurricanes, floods, wildfires, home fires, and other local disasters.

The Interview

Gail McGovern is obviously comfortable in her own skin, having nothing to prove to anyone. She's a woman who loves simply being who she is. Immediately likeable, she exudes warmth and friendliness, making a conversation with her both interesting and easy.

It became clear to me early in our interview that Gail's philanthropic bent was deeply influenced by her father, an optometrist who could be affectionately described as an "extreme" humanitarian who devoted much of his free time to volunteer efforts. Like her father, Gail seeks congruence, doing her best to live in accordance with the values she holds dear. It didn't take long to recognize Gail's priority in caring for people, whether it is her husband or daughter, the people with whom she works, or the populations she and her organization assist when a need arises. Hers is a life of service.

Though clearly a humanitarian and people person, Gail is no pushover. While people may be extremely important to her, she knows that the heart cannot dictate decisions made in a work context, as such decisions require a balance of both the head and the heart while determining what is best for the organization.

Gail McGovern doesn't try to make a square peg fit into a round hole. She has a deep respect for the knowledge and skills her employees bring to the table, evidenced by how she interacts with her team members individually or in meetings. Her passion and compassion ably drive the vision and mission she intends to reach, with an intricate balance of head and heart.

Pivotal Career Points

Early in her career, Gail McGovern showed signs of being adept at finding solutions, loving what she calls, *"complex puzzles to solve."* Driven by passion for her work, she set high performance standards for herself and is always in search of the next challenge. I perceive that one of her greatest cultivated leadership qualities was learning how to delegate in a way that served both employees and the organization. As a leader, Gail initially worried about being liked; this prompted a more indirect approach to getting things done. Not surprisingly, this approach was not always successful. In time, she learned to ask directly for what she wanted, making her expectations clear, succinct, and focused on desired results. It worked.

Another area in which Gail shines is staffing, finding and placing the right people on the team for the right reasons. During our interview she said, *"If you just staff for expediency, you will regret it."* Not only does she look for the best candidates, but the ones with the right chemistry who will work best with the rest of the leadership team. She makes sure she has a lineup of individuals who represent a diversity of thought and ideas. Her hiring process is painstaking because she is a self-described "softie" when it comes to people. She hates having to let somebody go. Thanks to having developed a knack for making the right hiring choices, she said, *"I haven't had to deal with performance problems in years."*

One of Gail McGovern's most notable accomplishments took place while she was at AT&T. At a time when 800 phone numbers were going portable, she became head of the toll-free numbers business. Gail knew she was taking on a job no one else wanted. Toll free numbers had never been portable, and AT&T had the largest market share of the 800 number trade. A lack of portability would hit AT&T hard if the company didn't make a timely change, a difficult maneuver for an organization of its size.

But Gail was confident in her abilities and that of her extraordinary team. Within 18 months, Gail and her team had revamped the entire 800 number business from A to Z—the advertising, sales strategy, and customer service. In the end, instead of an expected 10-point loss in business, AT&T lost only two points of its market share. Gail recounts, *"I had an incredible team. We loved working together. We were too naive to know that we'd signed on for an impossible task, and the outcome was stunning."*

Principles and Philosophy

Gail McGovern is an influential, far-thinking leader who has made a significant positive difference in the organizations where she has worked. Here is her personal and professional philosophy on the subject of leadership:

"I love talking about leadership. I think that leadership used to just mean charisma. Now, I think good leaders also have to demonstrate compassion and integrity. I believe really good leaders also need to have patience because results are not instantaneous. I also believe that there has to be a sense of inspiration so that people want to follow you, versus the idea that they have to follow you. This is quite a hefty list, and I don't want to give the impression that I excel in all of these. However, this list is what I use as my compass to lead this organization, as well as what guided the previous leadership roles I have played throughout my life.

One thing you should know about me is that I lead with humor. My staff meetings probably take twice as long as they should because everyone has a joke and we laugh together. I would say we have at least two belly laughs every half hour. I try to create an environment where, when the people come into my conference room, they have smiles on their faces because they are delighted to see each other; they laugh and feel happy about being at work. Let's face it, in this 24/7 world in which we live, you had better like your job, or else you are not going to like your life. To that end, I try to create an environment that is fun.

I have learned that when you have overachievers, you don't ever need to yell at them when they mess up because they are much, much harder on themselves than you could ever be. I will sit them down and I will say, 'Tell me what you did wrong.' They beat themselves up, and then I pat them on the back and say, 'You know what? You will make a better decision the next time you are faced with something like this.' I am not a yeller or screamer, but I encourage healthy debate. I encourage push back. When you staff great people, you don't really need to do much more than 'care and feed,' and let them do their thing."

Suggestions for Your Leadership Development

It was my pleasure to ask Gail McGovern her thoughts on what it takes for established and emerging leaders to be effective. This is what she told me:

"I always tell people that they need to be resilient, which sounds simple, but is hard. You absolutely will make mistakes, and how quickly you recover and course correct is what makes you a great leader, not the number of mistakes that you make.

When I would give my students at Harvard their big send-off and give them life advice, I would tell them that regardless of any career choice that they might make, they could always course correct. You really can do that. Fortunately, we don't live in a slave state, and if you make a mistake, you can undo it. You just have to do it quickly. I tell them they can always course correct from a career mistake.

Something that I was always very proud of was maintaining a work/life balance. This balance is essential to maintain your sanity, particularly for women. If you don't maintain work/life balance, demonstrating that you have a deep understanding of the fact that people are multi-dimensional, you are not going to be able to staff the best people. These two elements are very much linked. It was extremely important to me that I felt I was the one raising my daughter and didn't overly rely on nannies to raise her.

I am very proud of the fact that my nanny never worked a minute of overtime; either my husband or I were home by 7:00 every single night to make sure we were there to help with homework and to salve wounds if our daughter had a bad day socially. I would argue that my daughter turned out well. She is my proudest achievement, and I don't think that would have been possible with-out my husband and I maintaining some work/life balance.

My husband is my biggest supporter. I know when I lay out a problem that he will answer it in a way that has my best interest at heart. I lean very heavily on him and my brother, too, who is also my best friend. I also have a dear, dear friend who is almost like a sister, and she always gives great advice, as well. If you don't have someone to bounce off your woes, ideas, and thoughts, you are not going to be effective.

We tend to lead our lives like we can predict the course we will take and that we can control outcomes. What I have learned in life and in leadership is that life is actually an awkward journey and is not predictable. When you least expect it, someone is going to throw a curveball right at you, and it is probably going to hit you right in the head. What I have learned is that there are unex-pected times when you get that curveball thrown at you, and you need to lead with integrity and not act like you are freaking out.

Great leaders lead through diversity and adversity, not just in good times. The way you deal with adversity and life as a leader is really what makes you strong. Learning to have that feeling of being a little out of control can be very scary at times, but it usu-ally is developmental and often times fun."

CLOSING THOUGHTS

G ail McGovern seems the perfect blend of being both a task and people-oriented leader, possessing both business smarts and a compassionate heart. Imagine the pleasure of working with or for someone who doesn't cram square pegs into round holes or who makes sure that in every meeting there are at least two belly laughs every half hour? Besides the serious side of work, she knows the importance of making work fun.

As Mark Twain said, *"The human race has only one really effective weapon, and that is laughter. The moment it arises, our defenses melt and our irritations and resentments slip away, replaced by a moment where our spirits can shine."* We all know that when a sunny climate reigns in the workplace, productivity goes up. It's safe to say that Gail McGovern is masterful at generating a life-affirming atmosphere at work and in the organizations she leads. Not only are efficiency and effectiveness elevated, so are spirits.

--------- PROFILE ---------

Martha Mayhood Mertz

College of St. Catherine
BA, Michigan State University, Distinguished Alumni

Leader at a Glance

Local businesswoman whose *compelling vision and fortitude* established a *lasting legacy* in her personal crusade to challenge tradition and spotlight the value women authentically bring to the position of leadership.

Career Synopsis

Martha Mayhood Mertz—collaborator, advocate, and legacy builder—is a woman whose life's work took her by surprise. A highly successful real estate entrepreneur, she rose from local fame to globe-trotting author and speaker as the founder of ATHENA International, endorsing a new practice of leadership.

As a member of her local Chamber of Commerce board in the early 1980s, Martha recognized two needs: a call for more women leaders in the community, and for their voices to be heard. As the board's only female member, Martha worked closely and cooperatively with her male colleagues, demonstrating exemplary performance in her position so those around her could grasp the capabilities of women in a leadership position.

This was the genesis of ATHENA International, founded in 1982 by this dynamic woman who meticulously navigated her journey from local entrepreneur to international speaker and the mastermind founder of

ATHENA International. Martha serves on the ATHENA board and travels globally, sharing the message that women bring a distinctive, transforming approach to leadership—an approach that speaks to both male and female leaders of the 21st century.

Honors and Achievements

Martha Mayhood Mertz's organization supports, develops, and honors women leaders, making it impossible for women's leadership to be ignored. Now headquartered in Chicago, the thirty-five year-old ATHENA International has a global reach of over 7000 ATHENA recipients in more than 500 communities.

Martha's belief in, and value for, collaboration helped her build this well-known international organization. The ATHENA Leadership Award® honors women (or men) for professional excellence, community service, and the active assistance of helping women in their attainment of professional skills and outstanding leadership.

The Interview

My phone interview with Martha Mayhood Mertz was a joy. In listening to what she said and how she said it, her level of energy and focused comments confirmed that I was communicating with a woman who had mastered the art of being truly present. Martha listened intently during our conversation and responded to my questions thoughtfully and succinctly.

Talking with Martha felt like a conversation with a friend or colleague who shares a mutual interest in women's leadership. We discussed how the depth of experience women bring to their leadership roles makes it possible for them to wield influence at the highest levels. She spoke with a quiet passion about the importance of balancing male and female voices, outlining the advantages of women's authentic, collaborative approach to leadership and its positive impact on organizations.

If you are ever fortunate enough to meet Martha, you would note that she comes across as warm and friendly, but there's much more to this woman. She spoke with wisdom and self-confidence when describing female leaders and how they achieve success in distinctly different ways from the traditional male approach. She explained how those differences would prove valuable in the decades ahead as constant or unexpected change will demand organizational agility and flexibility at unprecedented levels.

Clearly, the ATHENA Award (named for the goddess) and what it stands for is an outgrowth of the value Martha places on women's innate (and cultivated) talents and what females naturally bring to leadership. Based on her generosity and openness during our interview, I sense that, in her presence, a leader at any level would feel valued.

From notable success in her local real estate business in the early 1980s to being the only woman on the Lansing Regional Chamber of Commerce board, Martha had a vision. After a year of learning how to "speak male," she began introducing board members to a different kind of leadership style, demonstrating the skills of enrolling and leading and getting others to create meaningful, valuable outcomes; all this without a formal leadership title or position. Here was the conundrum of the time: because most women were not yet holding *official* leadership titles or positions, they were not viewed as "leaders" or as having the potential to be leaders. Martha felt compelled to correct this gap and create a gender balance in leadership. And she succeeded.

Pivotal Career Points

As the lone female on the Lansing Regional Chamber of Commerce board, Martha saw the opportunity to create a board configuration more representative of her community. Blending collaboration with passion and canny insight, she carefully constructed a set of steps through which female leaders could achieve quantifiable goals so male colleagues would observe actual, measurable results. While this may seem obvious or extraneous in today's world, it was groundbreaking at the time.

The "plan" Martha crafted with a handpicked team (the future ATHENA Award) was so well conceived that nothing in its wording has been altered in over 25 years. While her original intention was only to benefit the local chamber, inspiration took over, and she resolved to take this model to a much larger stage. But before she could share her ideas on authentic leadership, Martha had to conquer her fear of speaking before groups. This was no easy feat.

Her fear of public speaking was a challenge Martha had to master, and this took time. She knew that to confidently expound on the importance of gender balance in leadership, she had to be completely comfortable expressing herself in a public forum. Progress was arduous, slow, and sometimes painful, but by drawing from her passion and vision, she perfected her presentation skills.

Principles and Philosophy

One leadership quality Martha finessed was a capacity for attracting the right kind of people to become a part of the ATHENA family—individuals who were able to identify resources and find funding; people who could carry on and make the organization grow far beyond its original vision. Had it not been for Martha's ability to attract such outstanding people along the way, ATHENA may never have expanded beyond its local roots and onto the international stage.

It was a pleasure meeting Martha on the phone and asking her to describe her personal and professional philosophy about leadership. If you had the pleasure and privilege to speak with this remarkable woman, here is what Martha Mayhood Mertz would tell you:

"Every effective leader has cultivated a number of skills. For me, number one is to be constantly learning. When a person becomes the fountain of knowledge—in other words, if they have reached the top and seem to be the primary source for everything— they often times will stop learning. But our world is moving so fast; if someone gives up on learning, the world will pass him or her by. We've identified that constant learning is one of the characteristics leaders must have in abundance.

Part of learning is mastering the art of listening. It isn't something you'd say is intuitively a leadership trait, but in ATHENA we found that effective leaders are marvelous listeners, and, because of this trait, they are learning constantly.

Perhaps the most important thing I have done to keep growing is continuing to understand my own values and how I am living my values, rather than simply speaking about them but not incorporating them into my life. Something I've seen in great leaders is a sense of self-knowing. They embody the words, 'To thine own self be true.'

49

If people aren't living what they say they believe, then they're not in harmony with themselves. Those who are not in harmony with themselves will not to be able to inspire others to follow them. In my efforts to stay in harmony, I try to make sure that the values I believe in are reflected in what I do every day. In ATHENA terms, we call it 'living authentically.'

When I'm part of a group of people and we are there to collaborate, everyone is valued, everyone is listened to, and everyone is heard. Sometimes ideas work and sometimes they don't. The fact is, you have these different voices coming together to achieve something in a truly collaborative effort. I think you bring out the best in people when they know their presence is valued."

Suggestions for Your Leadership Development

Here are the thoughts and suggestions Martha Mayhood Mertz offers to emerging and established leaders with an eye on advancing their careers:

"I want to tell women, 'Believe in yourself. Believe in your skills and talents and build upon them every chance you get. Don't try to become someone else. You have everything you need to carry yourself forward in life and achieve whatever your purpose might be.

Recognize that the definition of leadership is changing. We must no longer adhere to what I call the "male model" of leadership, which is more about command and control. This isn't the kind of leadership we need now, tomorrow, or fifty years from now. What we need right now are the quiet strengths we have found in the leaders who have become ATHENA recipients.'

I encourage any young woman, and man as well, to learn about these new models of leadership. Recognize that all of these things add up to leadership: listening and learning, caring about something enough to advocate fiercely, and having the courage when the occasion calls for it to stand up and tell the truth. Building relationships and collaborating and giving back of your time and talent is the new model. That's what we need to both recognize and celebrate.

Family members can be a great support system, though in some cases, they are not. Sometimes family members, inadvertently or intentionally, don't want to see someone succeed. I would suggest that if someone doesn't have a ready-made support system that they create one by making a family out of people who are mutually supportive. Everybody needs to be supported and encouraged. Encouragement from family helps to put things in a better balance. Adopt some sisters and brothers and choose them carefully. Build those relationships into trusting, caring, and mutually beneficial opportunities.

I used to think that if only I could look ahead twenty years and take a quick peek at what my world would look like, it would be so wonderful. But looking back now, I realize that it was so much better for me not to know and to simply grow daily and learn from what I was doing, both the positive and the negative. It was wonderful to have life unfold itself one day at a time. All has come in good time."

CLOSING THOUGHTS

As you can see, there is much to learn from Martha Mayhood Mertz, who, out of a desire to equalize a gender gap, became a tireless and passionate advocate for a new kind of leadership. Through her vision, courage, and fortitude, there now exists a balanced leadership model that blends the best of what males and females can bring to their vocations and avocations. Here is the ATHENA model of leadership, also discussed in detail in her book, *Becoming ATHENA, Eight Principles of Enlightened Leadership*:

- Living Authentically
- Building Relationships
- Giving back
- Fostering Collaboration
- Acting Courageously
- Learning Constantly
- Advocating Fiercely
- Celebration

Perhaps this model will inspire you to reach high, to drive your passion, be aligned, and lay the foundation of your path to success. May these values also ignite your fortitude and determination to help you forge ahead when the going gets tough.

The combination of these values and skills are yours for the taking. So is Martha's unwavering example. Who knows how far your reach may extend one day after you put these concepts into practice? Perhaps in the future you'll find yourself the subject of an interview by someone who admires your accomplishments. It's very possible that one day your personal and professional philosophy will be included in a book on accomplished women leaders. After all, stranger things have happened.

PROFILE

Naomi Rhode

2006 Honorary Doctorate, Central Pennsylvania College

Leader at a Glance

A born leader who rose to answer the call, *communicating vision* and *values*, setting standards for *excellence* in leadership on national and international levels.

Career Synopsis

Naomi Rhode is Co-Founder of SmartHealth, a multi-million-dollar company with extensive manufacturing sites in Asia, and divisions in eight countries. SmartHealth is a specialty company providing marketing and supply materials to the dental and medical professions.

Here we have a perfect example of how leadership comes in many forms—in this case, as an association volunteer: Naomi Rhode is Past President of the National Speakers Association and The Global Speakers Federation, the world body of professional speakers. Thanks to her saying *yes* to leadership, this internally aligned leader has now spoken in 50 states and 17 countries.

Honors and Achievements

Naomi's credentials include earning the CSP designation (Certified Speaking Professional), CSP Global Speaker, and receiving the CPAE (Council of Peers Award of Excellence) Speaker Hall of Fame, and the Cavett Award, all through the National Speakers Association. From the platform stage and small speaking venues alike, Naomi has inspired thousands of audience participants around the globe, sharing her expertise on leadership, interpersonal relationships, and life balance. In addition to being a much sought-after professional speaker, Naomi has authored three inspirational gift books and numerous anthologies. In addition to her speaking, writing, and active involvement in SmartHealth, she works as a transformational life coach, presentation skills consultant, and popular emcee.

The Interview

The term "bigger than life" may have been created for Naomi Rhode. Rooms seem to fill with her energy, and people sense that they are in the presence of someone significant. With her infectious smile and effervescent personality, she radiates charm and joie de vivre to everyone around her.

In all of my conversations with her, Naomi epitomized the image of a "gracious leader," a subject she discussed so fervently in her interview. Graceful and poised, she gave me her complete attention. As I watched her with others in social settings, she treated each person she spoke with as if they were the only person in the room. Her personal attention—her presence—invites people to feel important and valued. That, I believe, is one of her greatest gifts.

Naomi was born into a family where leadership and authority were respected and integrity was valued. Within this family, Naomi experienced, first-hand, models of personal leadership and the positive differences an effective leader could make. Challenged from the time she was a child to become all that she was called to be, she was naturally drawn toward leadership roles from grade school on, becoming president of every organization to which she belonged.

During her many years of involvement with the National Speakers Association, in ascending to the presidency, Naomi says that she *"fell in love with members of the board and the process and purpose"* of leading her treasured association. From there, Naomi Rhode led the Global Speakers Federation as well. Among other worthy lessons gleaned during her lifetime of assuming leadership positions, Naomi learned the power of collaboration and the importance of selecting the best-of-the-best to be part of her leadership teams.

Throughout her career, Naomi learned to take risks, recognizing that leadership is not a one-time event, but a lifetime of learning. Although risk is ongoing in the business world with her company SmartHealth, Naomi looks to her volunteer leadership positions for some of her greatest lessons.

Pivotal Career Points

For example, during her presidential year with the National Speakers Association, Naomi felt that her biggest risk was in selecting a strong, forceful person who would be in charge of all the major meetings. As a wise leader, she took the risk of being upstaged or overshadowed by this powerful personality. But selecting the best chairperson and the best leaders during her presidency paid off handsomely by benchmarking some of the grandest, most memorable conferences and conventions in the history of the organization.

One of Naomi's most notable accomplishments as NSA president was her willingness to reach out to members. Believing it was critical for her to be acquainted with as many NSA members as was possible, Naomi chose to speak at every state chapter during her tenure. Similarly, as president of the Global Speakers Federation, she visited every country, traveling at her own expense, wherever an association existed. Because of her dedication to the members she served, Naomi gave her all, expecting nothing in return but friendship and connection. She became intimately acquainted with members around the world at a face-to-face, hand-to-hand, hug-to-hug level, making friendships that will last a lifetime.

In the five years spanning her national and global presidencies, Naomi dictated and typed over 2000 letters, determined not to lead in a remote fashion. If you wrote to her, you would get a letter back. If you did something nice for her, you received an acknowledgment. She was committed to taking photos and sending them out, doing whatever she could to keep in touch. Every day she called at least one member, at random, to say, *"Hey, Naomi Rhode here. I'm just so privileged to be president of our association this year. I want to know how your business is going, and how you are doing."* These are examples of a leader who didn't merely want the idea of staying connected; she spent the money and time to do so.

Naomi told me that her going above and beyond wasn't just for others. She did it to improve her skills as a leader and to fully enjoy her time as

president of the association. She wanted to look back on her presidencies as the richest periods in her entire life, explaining that in giving to
others, we bless ourselves.

Principles and Philosophy

As with the corporate leaders I interviewed, I asked Naomi Rhode to share
her perspective and views on leadership:

*"My perspective on leadership has changed over the years in an
almost frightening way. When you are at the helm, you recognize
what Robert Frost meant in his poem about the two roads diverg-
ing in a yellow wood. You make a decision as to which road to
take, and you can never go back. You realize that the leader, the
person you put at the helm, the captain of the ship, is going to take
you where he or she plans to go.*

*I now have much more respect for government officials, for the
whole political process in our country—how and why we elect our
presidents, who then go on to appoint Supreme Court justices and
other officials. That whole leadership picture to me is so much more
awe-filled than it was before. I took it for granted before, but I don't
anymore, and I have much more respect for those in leadership.*

*If I were to identify the number one thing I believe contributed
to my success, it would be the sovereignty of God. I believe the Creator of the Universe knew who I would be before the foundations
of the earth and directed my plans. I do not have any doubt about
that. That is number one.*

*But I was placed in an amazing family. My father and mother
were both giants in their own work. They died when I was still very
young, but I still received so much from them. My dad died when
I was thirteen and my mother when I was just twenty-three. I still
think about them almost every day, which rather amazes me. I still
remember their 'mother messages' and 'father messages.'*

*Balance between home life and work is huge. Fortunately, for
me, the way we chose to do it worked out well. We married young
and were young when we had our babies, so we were in our early
forties when they were off to college. That left a good 20 to 30*

years for me to be on the platform and to travel for my speaking engagements without any restrictions. Actually, I have been on an airplane almost every week for almost forty years.

The exception was when I had a major stroke in 2008 on my way to a speech at the Grand Hotel on Mackinac Island in Michigan; I ended up spending a month in a hospital in Traverse City. Obviously, I had to take some time off to recuperate. I am still speaking only about half the time, but have started a speaker's life coaching business. I have a good client base and just love it.

I can be a transformational life coach because of my vast experience, and this has opened up a whole new profession for me. I can now use coaching at this point of my life to augment the speaking I am still doing."

Suggestions for Your Leadership Development

For every leader featured in this book, there is unique story and path that each woman chose. When I asked Naomi Rhode what advice, thoughts, or suggestions she would give to established and emerging leaders, this is what she told me:

"If you have been consistent at being a leader in your business, your chosen profession, your community, your church, or in any of the venues that you engage in, you have built a wealth of knowledge, but you may have no idea that you have it. Monitor your experiences. Remember them. Stay aware of all the lessons you learn and the skills you have cultivated.

To continue improving as a leader and human being, my recommendation is to read, read, read. My advice to women leaders is to take risks, to join interests of your heart, and volunteer in professional associations, saying yes often! One thing leads to another. Experience and education are never wasted; they accumulate to provide you with the knowledge and skills you need for the next challenge."

CLOSING THOUGHTS

In reading Naomi Rhode's interview, I was again reminded of the power of working with *excellence* and with a *joyful heart*— two qualities that define this authentic woman. As a long-time member of the National Speakers Association, I have witnessed Naomi's leadership first-hand, and have observed congruence in her actions and beliefs. It's not what a leader professes that creates loyal followers, but rather what others discern from her being, from what speaks silently about her character, commitment, and contribution. And, it is by Naomi Rhode's actions that I have come to know her as a leader among the best-of-the-best.

I do not know if Naomi Rhode ever met Mary Kay Ash, founder of Mary Kay Cosmetics, but no one epitomizes Mary Kay's philosophy any better than Naomi: *"We treat our people like royalty. If you honor and serve the people who work for you, they will honor and serve you."* Naomi has spent a lifetime honoring and serving the people who work for her and with her, and, in return, she has received honor and service from them.

Naomi Rhode has been unstoppable because of her belief that she was put here to become all that she was called to be, and she rose to the challenge. I hope that her unrelenting drive to make the most of her gifts and talents in service to others will inspire you to greater heights through a pursuit of excellence, desire for relationship, and a yearning to serve in whatever capacity you choose as your life's work.

PROFILE

Mary Ellen Rodgers

BS, Bowling Green University

Leader at a Glance

A dedicated *relationship builder* and strategic thinker whose unflagging *commitment* resulted in building a cohesive remote international team.

Career Synopsis

Mary Ellen Rodgers is Deloitte LLP's U.S. Managing Partner for Workplace Services. Responsible for nearly 4,000 employees across more than 150 offices, she has had far-reaching influence throughout the organization over the past several years. Serving in a number of capacities throughout her leadership journey, Mary Ellen was Partner-in-Charge of the Audit and Enterprise Risk Services for the Michigan offices, numbering close to 500 client services professionals. As managing partner of the practice in West Michigan, she was responsible for all aspects of the practices of nearly 100 professionals.

In her role as Officer of Deloitte LLP's Corporate and Social Responsibility, her energies were focused on Ethics and Compliance, Talent, Community Involvement, and Client Services through Enterprise Sustainability. Mary Ellen also served as the National Director of Deloitte's Initiative for the Retention and Advancement of Women, where she was responsible for implementing programs in career growth, mentoring, leadership development, gender awareness, and balancing multiple commitments. Her role was communicating and introducing change to the firm by meeting the business imperative of advancing and retaining women. But as impressive as this list of credits may sound, there's more.

Honors and Achievements

Besides an incredibly active work life with myriad responsibilities, Mary Ellen has been active in the community. She served as the chairperson on a number of boards, most notably, Board of Directors of Heart of West Michigan United Way, Frederik Meijer Gardens, YMCA of Greater Grand Rapids, and St. John's Home. Mary Ellen has been recognized as one of the 50 Most Influential Women in West Michigan numerous times and as a YWCA Woman of Achievement and a Michigan Woman of Achievement and Courage.

The Interview

Stately and impressive, with red hair and an expansive smile, Mary Ellen Rodgers presented a striking figure as she stepped into the conference room for our interview. Radiating an aura of self-assured calmness, her tall, commanding presence filled the room with energy. There was something captivating about her vibrant manner and clear, concise speech that compelled me to catch her every word. As the interview progressed, it became obvious that this woman is completely congruent and authentic, clearly knowing what she brings to her organization and those who work for her. I sensed that I was in the presence of someone in total harmony with her inner self.

Her leadership journey is equally fascinating. An adventurous risk taker and intentional relationship builder, Mary Ellen let it be known at a somewhat early age that she was ready to step into a significant leadership position. Understanding the importance of demonstrating *why* she should move up in the organization, Mary Ellen's hard work and dedication to excellence, both in task and with people, was instrumental in her career flourishing. Her decision making process may be more straightforward than most, for she clearly understands her priorities and resolves herself to action with those priorities in mind. As I listened to this approachable, bright, and capable woman's story, I couldn't help but think, *"She is a true leader!"*

Mary Ellen not only worked hard and vigorously, but she regularly talked with her manager about the results she was getting and the goals she was accomplishing. She continually asked herself, *"How did I just help the organization be successful?"* When she described the results to her manager, it wasn't a matter of blowing her own horn, but getting into the habit of reporting successful achievement of goals. Over time, her results and successes got noticed, making it easier to continue moving forward. Mary Ellen believes that objectively reporting accomplishments and the value they bring to the organization is a critical skill for women who desire greater responsibility.

Another notable leadership quality Mary Ellen possesses is her genuine caring for her people. She understands the importance of connecting at a personal level, building the right team, and being authentic in her interactions by demonstrating that she cares for others. As a result, people trust that she is telling the truth and that she is doing what she believes is best for them and the broader organization. Her emphasis on caring about people is evident through her personal beliefs and the advice she gives those who are seeking bigger assignments and more responsibility.

Pivotal Career Points

In addition to her impressive credentials with Deloitte, what I consider one of Mary Ellen's notable accomplishments was her willingness to accept—and succeed—in a job for which she had had no formal education or experience. This is the position she still holds today. When the firm's managing partner asked her to take on such monumental responsibilities, she found it somewhat shocking being asked to take on something she'd never given a thought to doing.

In sharing the proposal with her father, he said, *"Oh, my gosh! You know nothing about this. How can you ever be successful in a role you know nothing about? Procurement, real estate, world security—these are not the normal assignments that an audit partner with an accounting degree would do well at."* Mary Ellen suddenly realized she didn't have to have all the answers. She knew she'd be surrounded with an impressively knowledgeable team who would help her figure things out. Saying *yes* to this daunting position was the defining moment that led to the role she enjoys today. For me, the courageous part of her decision to take on such responsibility was in realizing that the leader doesn't need to know all of the answers, but needs to trust in her team who has much to offer.

I also admire how Mary Ellen nurtured her spirit and aligned and strengthened her character, trusting in what she calls her personal *"North Star,"* using her true north as a guide for making decisions; for when to say yes or no. One such decision was personal. She described the value she placed on watching her son play varsity football because it was important to him that she showed up for his games. Therefore, Friday night football was always a priority. The only thing that would keep her away was an emergency.

There were other times when work took priority. For one of the seventh grade parent/teacher conferences, Mary Ellen found she would be working in India. Unable to accompany her husband to the parent/teacher conference, she arranged her schedule so she could call her son Daniel after he and his father returned from the school so she could get the low-down directly from her son.

Mary Ellen has found that nurturing that deeper part of her (staying true to her personal North Star), helps her avoid wasting a lot of time and energy over conflicted feelings about work or personal decisions. She finds the clarity very freeing.

Principles and Philosophy

As with each of the unstoppable women profiled in this book, I was eager to hear Mary Ellen Rodgers talk about her personal and philosophical viewpoint. Here is what she told me about her perspective on leadership and strategies for growing an effective team, even when people are scattered around the world:

"As a young professional, I believed that leadership was more about position and power, and the ability to make decisions. Today, I think leadership really has nothing to do with position. It has everything to do with influence. How do you influence your team and others in the organization? How do you influence people so they at least have an open mind for listening to your ideas and strategies? It takes a very different leadership style; one that I believe creates more success today than it did 25 years ago when

I started in the business. No one really cares what my title is and most people probably don't know what it means. Certainly the 3500 plus people who work within my part of the organization are more concerned about how I can help influence them to have a better career, an easier work day, and better relationships with their internal clients.

When leading a team remotely, you have to incorporate some personal connectivity. That doesn't mean you need to be best friends with everybody, but you need to respect each other's philosophies and judgment. While you can do that through e-mail and instant messaging, or over the phone, oftentimes not being face-to-face becomes a great challenge.

Right after I took on this new role in the firm, the economy situation caused the firm to put a ban on travel. I had no direct reports set within my geographic area. My direct reports were spread from the West Coast to New York, from Miami to India. Since I believe that creating 'connective tissue' is so important in a well-functioning team, I really needed to look for opportunities, cues, and small signs on how to connect. I had to find out what was important to the people on my team, and relate to them through services like Instant Messenger.

So if somebody says, 'I am going to miss a phone call because my mother is sick,' I remember three days later to send a quick instant message that says, 'I hope your mother is feeling better.' Or if somebody says, 'I am struggling with an issue in my team,' I pick up the phone and say, 'Let me just offer you what I have done in the past. Maybe that will be helpful to you.' This is a different way of team building than walking the halls, stopping at people's office doors, and having a normal lunch break or cup of coffee."

Suggestions for Your Leadership Development

As with every outstanding leader featured in this book, Mary Ellen Rodgers offered some clear and doable ideas for both established and emerging leaders in today's work world:

"I advise the women I mentor to look for opportunities to stand

*out. For example, when I go around the country and do roundta-
ble discussions with people, and I say, 'Alright guys, you can ask
me anything,' usually the first person to ask a question is the person who becomes memorable to me. To me, the one who is willing
to speak out is someone who looks for opportunities. That's what I
mean by the one who stands out, who takes risks, asks the question,
or seeks clarification. Be the one who walks up and shakes someone's hand within the organization that you don't know. Putting
your head down and doing the work is good, but it is not enough
to take you to the next level, partly because it doesn't give you the
ability to build those relationships.*

*I am always very impressed when someone raises a hand and
asks a question about something that is very topical. It doesn't need
to be an overly complex question; it could be something as easy
as, 'I read in this week's newsletter that you mentioned such-and-
such. Can you talk a little bit more about that?' It doesn't mean you
know a lot about it, but from my perspective, I think, 'Wow, this
is somebody who takes her career seriously and has actually read
the newsletter, or the strategy document, or whatever it may be.'*

*It's also very important to have a support system. My schedule
is very hectic, and when I took this job, my husband decided that
he would stay home with the children. For us, spending time with
the children was important, and that was something he decided
to do. It has worked very well for us. A big part of my support is
knowing that my husband is taking care of a lot of things that,
quite frankly, I don't need to worry about. This is something you
can't take for granted.*

*I think it's important to find people you can call when you're
having a bad day and say, 'You know what, I am going to have
my game face on all day, but I just really need somebody I can
vent to, I need a shoulder to cry on, or I just need five minutes of
conversation about something totally silly to help me get my mind
in a different place.' You'll find these people in odd places: a person on a board in the community whom you just have a fondness
for; someone you have influenced, maybe not even in a direct way;
someone you have worked with; someone with whom you have an*

affinity, and with whom you really feel that you can have those types of conversations. Everyone needs somebody who says, 'Yes, you can do it,' and 'Yes, I will help you figure out this particular issue or problem.'

I tell young women (including my niece who has just entered the work force as an attorney) not to come in with preconceived notions in terms of what is possible and what is not possible. Break down your career into manageable pieces. Take time every year to sit down and ask yourself, 'What have I learned? How am I better? What are the things that I still need to learn? How do I put myself in a position of not being stagnant, but truly growing in ways that are important to me and important to creating that leadership style that I aspire to?'"

CLOSING THOUGHTS

There is no question that Mary Ellen Rodgers has what it takes to be successful, not just in her chosen field, but also in arenas where she had no formal education. She simply has that certain something that all great leaders seem to possess—an ability to see beyond the immediate and obvious to what *can be*. She has that ability to overcome those things that stop others in their tracks.

Edmund Hillary, one of the first to reach the summit of Mount Everest, wrote, *"It is not the mountain we conquer but ourselves."* In looking over my interview with Mary Ellen Rodgers, one could argue that those words were written for Mary Ellen Rodgers. In fact, some of what I consider her greatest accomplishments are deeply personal, but truth be told, it is our personal beliefs (and conquests) that drive our leadership behaviors.

──────── PROFILE ────────

Ruth Shaw

MA, East Carolina University
Ph.D., University of Texas, Austin

Leader at a Glance

Intentional learner and *internally aligned* servant leader who unintentionally parlayed her academic credentials and community service *contributions* into unprecedented success within a male-dominated industry.

Career Synopsis

Ruth Shaw distinguished herself as a leader in community college education and civic organizations in an "organic" manner, advancing to senior executive roles in industries traditionally held exclusively by males. Destined for leadership, Ruth has served and continues to serve on many boards, including Southwire Company, DTE Energy, The Dow Chemical Company, and the board of trustees of the University of North Carolina at Charlotte where she serves as chair.

Honors and Achievements

Through local leadership roles she held as President of Central Piedmont Community College, Ruth came to know the chairman and vice chairman of (then) Duke Power Company. Working shoulder-to-shoulder with these individuals while focusing on important community issues, she was offered a leadership position at Duke Power, where she served as Vice President of Corporate Communications, Senior Vice President of Corporate Resources, and Chief Administrative Officer.

In 1997, Ruth moved over to serve the parent company, Duke Energy, as Executive Vice President and Chief Administrative Officer. In 2003, she became the President of Duke Power and in 2004, she added the title of CEO. Two years later she became the Group Executive for Public Policy and President of Duke Nuclear.

Ruth Shaw epitomizes every working woman's dream, achieving as perfect a work-life balance as is achievable. She actively and rigorously prioritized her work and personal life. Knowing there was so much she wanted to accomplish, and given that there are only so many hours in a day, she knew it would be impossible to do it all unless she closely monitored what she did and when. From self-management to careful selection of models and mentors, Ruth consistently clarified what was most important to her and focused her efforts on achieving tangible results in each of these priority areas.

The Interview

Ruth Shaw immediately struck me as a woman who embodies the concept of *Southern charm*. Warm and genteel, I found her immensely likeable. Ruth spoke with ease and confidence, exuding a strong sense of being at peace with herself, her life, and her accomplishments. While she came across as a woman who would take her work very seriously, I would describe Ruth as someone who is also able to laugh at herself and who, while taking pride in her achievements, would be humble enough to admit her mistakes.

Ruth's success is largely based on her authenticity, her insistence on simply being herself. She learned early on in her leadership journey that trying hard to be someone or something that you are not is most often a recipe for failure. She also proactively sought out and learned from mentors throughout her professional life. She was smart enough to figure out when particular advice was no longer working for her, and she sought new mentors when it seemed appropriate.

I asked Ruth about mentors and any lessons she learned from them. She shared an amusing, yet memorable story from early on in her career when she interviewed for a job with Bill Priest, Chancellor of the Dallas County Community College District. Ruth shares this as a lesson on authenticity with all of the women she mentors.

"When I went to interview for the job I was in my twenties. This was a dean's job, Academic VP of the college. I was hopelessly unprepared for that position based on my experience, and everybody told me that I needed to look older, needed to look older, needed to look older and, believe me, by the time I got there, I was MUCH older. I wore a very frumpy suit, I had my very wild hair pinned down in sort of a bun and carried an umbrella. In spite of all that, we had a good interview.

When I left his office, Bill sort of gave me this up and down look and said, 'Tell me, do you always dress that way?' And I said, 'Well, no, as a matter of fact, I don't.' And he said, 'Well you never need do it again on my account.' It was a wonderful lesson about being who you are. I was completely myself in the conversation, but I had listened to all that outside noise that said I had to look older, and it didn't fool anybody. That was the first of many, many lessons I learned from him, but it was probably one of the most important."

It might be argued that Ruth Shaw was *born to serve.* Even as a young girl she envisioned herself serving in positions of leadership, convinced that she had what it took to lead: confidence, competence and a willingness to step forward when a job needed to be done. Though she lost her bid for governor at Girls' State, she forged ahead, putting herself forward for the office of lieutenant governor and won.

Ruth knew she wanted to be a leader in the field of education and pursued her Ph.D. to prepare herself for the opportunity. She worked hard to build a career, a social network, and competence within the community college leadership environment. A committed learner, she continuously worked to develop her knowledge and skills while cultivating her social connections as she stepped forward to serve her community. It didn't take long for her to be noticed by those in the business arena.

Pivotal Career Points

Ruth's advances in academia were intentional, but not so with her move into business. As she explained, *"I was simply out to do good work on behalf of the community."* When the vice chair of Duke Power asked to meet with her, she thought it was to discuss another charitable or civic endeavor. His asking her to become part of Duke Power's leadership team came as a complete surprise.

In following Ruth Shaw's career, consider her extraordinary ability at such a young age to focus her energies on a future of her own choosing. Where many young women give little or no thought to their futures, Ruth Shaw had already mapped out her path, developing the skills, competencies, and connections required for success. Early on, she set into motion the wheels that would propel her toward a journey of influence, service, and opportunities even she had never have imagined. As a result, she has had the good fortune to make significant and meaningful contributions to society. Indeed, she has made a difference, not only for others, but herself as well.

Ruth's servant heart, her ardent preparation, and unstoppable faith in the ability of others to generously contribute to projects ultimately paved the way for her leadership development. From the beginning, Ruth believed she could succeed regardless of the setting. She knew she had the capacity to learn, and she sensed that with the help and the collaboration of others, she could thrive in any setting. Clearly, she was correct in her self-assessment.

Ruth Shaw may never have considered personal contentment as a major accomplishment, but it speaks volumes about how she has lived her life. During our interview, she mentioned that later in her career when she was leading large organizations, she did not cultivate deep, long-lasting relationships with women as she had earlier in life; women who are still her best friends. Instead, Ruth chose to sacrifice new friendships for the sake of higher priorities. What discretionary "relationship" time she had went to her husband, her two sons, and her mother, the four most important people in her life.

Though she realizes that every choice comes with a cost, Ruth has no regrets. She was always clear on her priorities and doing what really mattered. Freely admitting she still cannot cook or sew, and is not a particularly good hostess, she now enjoys exploring these and other activities, regardless of whether or not she's good at them. Throughout her life, Ruth has made conscious choices based on priorities, and though sometimes she wishes she had cultivated more friends from later in her career, she would not change a thing. Her clarity stands as an impressive model to consider.

Principles and Philosophy

As for her personal and professional philosophy, not surprisingly, Ruth was very clear on her thoughts about what she wants and expects from others and herself:

"I run from people who aren't truth-worthy. That sounds simple, but it pays to diligently avoid people you can't count on to tell you the truth. Positions of leadership become very vulnerable when people begin to tell you what you want to hear, or what they think you want to hear. I want people I can trust to be straight with me and obviously people who, once the decision is made, will follow me. I want their best thinking, their toughest critique when we are a team or when it's just the two of us in a learning situation.

I want the best, most solid feedback I can get. If you're not trustworthy in that fundamental way, then I will run from you as fast as I can. To me this issue reflects on a lot of other things. It reflects on your authenticity as a human being and how you generally treat other people. It means the difference between being more of a self-promoter than a servant leader.

When building my teams, I looked for people who had deep competence in leadership and management, and I mean that in a broad view as well as special expertise. I looked for people who were in one way or another stronger or better than I was, people from whom I could learn; people who were team players. I intentionally built a team instead of select individuals. I tried to work at complementary skills sets and I looked unerringly for people who had a strong sense about valuing others, about collaboration, and about being a team player. I didn't get it right in every case, but I think I did the best job of putting together a high functioning, high performance team in that world."

Suggestions for Your Leadership Development

When I asked Ruth Shaw about what she would say to emerging leaders about taking responsibility for their own success, here is what she said:

"For me it's always tough to inspire someone else unless you are good at motivating yourself. When you look at your career and any position that you hold, there is a paradoxical statement that is true: It's not about you and it's all about you. Here is what I mean. You really have to take responsibility for yourself. The personal competence, confidence, skills and connections that you develop are yours; they belong to you, all of them. When you leave that job and go to another one, or you leave that job to stay home, you will take those skill sets, those relationships, that history of what you did with you.

But it's also not about you, and you will never realize that more until you are in a position like president or CEO or some other senior position, and one day you leave that job and the lights don't even flicker. A lot goes with the position itself, and it is NOT about you. It is about the authority, the power, and the connections that that position holds. So, try to stay clear in your own mind about the difference. Nurture those things that are all about you and respect those things that go with the position itself."

CLOSING THOUGHTS

As the saying goes, *she had me at hello.* From the moment I met Dr. Ruth Shaw over the phone, it was clear this woman had the gift of putting others instantly at ease. Her natural love of people oozed from every pore, not so much in what she said, but in who and what she is, a woman of excellence who came not to be served, but to serve.

Sometimes we have the tendency to think that a woman who has reached the pinnacle of power in what was traditionally a man's world—the Energy Industry—would come across as rather sober. Quite the opposite is true of Ruth Shaw. She is every bit as feminine and charming, really, as you would expect from Southern hospitality.

Her sense of humor comes through when she tells on herself, clearly not taking herself too seriously. What she does take seriously is the importance of serving the community and the organizations she's been honored to serve. My hope is that the depth and breadth of the character of this woman, along with her experiences and her legacy, come across on the written page and inspire you to become all that you were intended to be. By example, Ruth Shaw set the standard for all of us. Be yourself and believe in yourself. Stay true to your priorities. Be a person of integrity. Be all these things and others will notice.

PROFILE

Mary Ellen Sheets

Michigan State University

Leader at a Glance

A self-proclaimed "accidental entrepreneur" who *believed in herself* enough to seek her *passion* with persistence and courage, founding and growing the highly successful company, Two Men and a Truck.

Career Synopsis

Mary Ellen Sheets left her systems analyst job with the State of Michigan in 1989, foregoing security and her retirement, to pursue her dream of creating a thriving business. Helping her sons in their after-school moving venture, she entered a field devoid of and not particularly welcoming to women. In time, this little local family enterprise grew into a national and, eventually, an international franchise.

Today, Two Men and A Truck has grown to 2,100 trucks and employs over 8,000 employees from 39 states in the US with more than 330 locations worldwide, including Canada, Ireland, and the United Kingdom. Two Men and a Truck holds the distinction of being the nation's largest franchised moving company with sales of over $300 million annually.

Honors and Achievements

Here is a sampling of accolades and awards Mary Ellen has received: Michigan Entrepreneur of the Year Award, Michigan Business Woman of the

Year, Ernst & Young International Runner-up Entrepreneur of the Year, Entrepreneur of the Year by the International Franchise Association, Athena Award, Michigan Women's Foundation Women of Achievement and Courage Award, Working Women's 500 Congress, Working Women's Best Employer Regional Finalist. And there are more.

Mary Ellen has been featured on the Oprah Winfrey Show, Business-Week Online, The Detroit Free Press, National Enquirer, and NBC's Today. Though now retired from the business, Mary Ellen currently serves on the boards of the International Franchise Association, the Lansing Chamber of Commerce, Sparrow Hospital in Lansing, and Michigan Chamber of Commerce, to name a few.

The Interview

If you had the pleasure of meeting Mary Ellen Sheets, you might easily mistake her for a career homemaker who delights in domestic activities such as baking cookies or knitting booties for her grandkids. Though I knew ahead of time I'd be meeting a savvy businesswoman, this warm-hearted, easygoing woman who is "so much who she is," feels no need or compulsion to impress anyone with her credentials. Truth be told, Mary Ellen is indeed congenial and homey; talking with her is like chatting with a friend, sharing a cup of coffee at the kitchen table. Her unpretentious manner invites you to immediately feel comfortable, as she unhesitatingly and openly discusses both challenges and successes in her work and personal life.

Modestly downplaying the role she played in the growth of the company, Mary Ellen credits her daughter, Melanie Bergeron (current chairperson), for its stunning success. With a blend of humility and self-deprecating humor, Mary Ellen isn't teasing when she calls herself an *"accidental entrepreneur."* In reading her remarkable story, you get a sense of this leader's kind and loving nature and the depth to which she values and affirms her connections with people.

Mary Ellen Sheets, self-made businesswoman, community volunteer, and philanthropist, came to high-level leadership in a most unexpected way. Taking over the small moving business her sons had started before they went off to college, she stepped into a world looming with unknowns.

Pivotal Career Points

Despite her extreme shyness, this plucky woman overcame her fears and met them head-on. Regardless of her discomfort, she forced herself to attend social and networking events where she would meet and connect with strangers, handing out business cards and building alliances. She labored long and hard at learning everything she needed to know about the moving business and the daunting number of laws regulating the industry.

Despite her initial reservations, Mary Ellen never allowed failure to unnerve her. She kept learning, trusting her instincts, and picking herself up when needed, while continually moving forward with enthusiasm and fervor. An incurable optimist, when her attorney announced that she had just sold her tenth franchise (the critical indicator that her business was an undeniable success), she wasn't surprised. Driven by passion and the love of something she could call her own, it never occurred to Mary Ellen that she might fail in her quest. Imagine the strength of mind it takes to be so focused and determined.

Among her many leadership qualities is her huge, loving heart. Mary Ellen has always been generous with both her time and financial resources, giving where and when there's a need, whether individuals, community agencies, or causes in which she wholeheartedly believes. The value for giving back has been an integral part of her business practice since the early days.

With the first $1,000 she made in the moving business, Mary Ellen sat down and wrote out ten checks for $100 each, designated for local charities. This giving philosophy is an innate, organic part of her company culture. Each year, franchise locations donate thousands of hours and dollars to the non-profit organizations of their choice. Additionally, every move that is completed by Two Men and a Truck involves a donation to the American Cancer Society.

That Mary Ellen Sheets, a single mom who raised three kids, rose from humble beginnings to build an international moving franchise is, in my mind, a stunningly notable feat. How many women can claim such a daunting achievement? Despite the hard work and many challenges along the way, she believed in her abilities and never lost hold of her desire to create a better life for herself and her children.

Driven by passion, compelled by her vision and mission, she grew the company step by step. Mary Ellen was always willing to not only do whatever it took to learn what was needed, but actually to do whatever it took to succeed, all the time knowing that her first loyalty was to her children. By example and practice, she passed along to her daughter and sons the values of faith, family, and service.

Mary Ellen successfully raised three talented, well-educated, and hard-working children, all of whom work together harmoniously in the family business. Daughter Melanie Bergeron is Chairperson, son Brig Sorber is CEO, and son Jon Sorber is Executive Vice President. Though Mary Ellen is officially retired from the business, she still owns part of the company along with her children, and all decisions are still made as a family.

Principles and Philosophy

I am confident you'll find Mary Ellen's personal and professional philosophy as refreshingly simply and wise as I do. Here is what this remarkable woman had to say.

"The overall lesson I learned as a new business owner was not to listen to negative people. When you start a business, stick to your guns. Go with your gut feeling. Do something you really want to do. Life is not a dress rehearsal. Give back. Treat people well. There's something we call 'The Grandma Rule' for the company. It says: 'Treat everyone the way you want your grandma treated.' I think that it is a great motto and applies to a lot of other things in life, too.

To bring out the best in every employee, I think you need to show him or her that you can do the hard work, too, and that you will work right beside them. They need to know you're all working together. I like transparency. Our franchise system is unique in that we share all the figures. Everyone knows how much everyone else makes, how much is spent on tires and other expenses, and how much they pay all their people. Everything is open. We operate that way because that's how we started. I simply didn't know that businesses didn't do things that way."

Suggestions for Your Leadership Development

When I asked Mary Ellen Sheets what words of advice she would offer to emerging leaders and women who want to have a lasting influence on others, here is what she said:

> *"As a leader in business, it is very important to show compassion for everyone. If one of your people suffers a loss, if there is a funeral for example, do everything you can to make sure you get there. During a bad time, when people need help, make sure you are there. If you can make it to a wedding, that's always nice, but sad times are the most important times to show support.*
>
> *I don't come into the office much anymore because I am retired. But I find out online when people have babies, and I like to buy a bunch of baby things and bring them in just to show that I care about their families. We have always had office picnics where employees bring their kids or dogs, and I get to know them all.*
>
> *It's important to personally show you care for people around you. Always put others first. If it is your customers or your employees, try to think and do everything the best way you can for them, so you'll have good outcomes."*

CLOSING THOUGHTS

I n our conversation, I couldn't help but think that a good deal of the impressive success Mary Ellen Sheets has enjoyed is connected to her basic values of kindness, concern, and consideration for other people's feelings. From that single mom turned accidental entrepreneur to respected and established international businesswoman, she never compromised her value for family in her journey toward success.

Nor did she surrender to the initial fears that could have prevented her from making her mark in this world. Perhaps you'll keep her optimistic nature in mind when or if you feel overwhelmed by circumstances that intimidate or challenge your mission and vision. Stifle your doubts, believe in yourself, and step by step, keep learning and moving toward your dream so that one day you'll be an inspiration for others, just like Mary Ellen.

PROFILE

La June Montgomery Tabron

BBA, University of Michigan
MBA, Kellogg Graduate School of Management
at Northwestern University
Honorary Doctorate of Humane Letters, Marygrove College, Detroit, MI
Honorary Doctorate of Humane Letter, Union Institute & University

Leader at a Glance

A bridge builder, philanthropist, and *woman of integrity* who realized her *vision* of making a difference for children, families, and communities, prevailing against all odds in a traditional, male-dominated institution.

Career Synopsis

La June Montgomery Tabron, President and CEO of the W.K. Kellogg Foundation, is a certified public accountant and certified management accountant who began her career as foundation controller in 1987. She served as the executive vice president of operations and treasurer before being named CEO in 2014. Her advocacy for empowering youth spans a wide range of programs, from those in her hometown Detroit, to those in communities in Mississippi, New Mexico, and New Orleans.

Honors and Achievements

La June is a woman of firsts. She was the first person of color to be hired for a permanent professional position at the W.K. Kellogg Foundation in its 84-year history. She is the first female and first African American woman to become its president and CEO. La June played an active leadership role in the Kellogg Foundation's first racial equity, diversity, and inclusion effort for more than two decades, internally with board and staff, and externally with grantees and community partners. In 2015, La June received the Courageous Leader Award from White Men as Full Diversity Partners (WMFDP). The award recognizes courageous leaders who forge tangible and transformative shifts in the way diversity and inclusion is practiced in their organization.

La June sat on the board of the Western Michigan University Foundation and Battle Creek Community Health Partners, and chaired the Battle Creek Health Systems Board. She is actively involved in a number of other local boards and committees.

The Interview

In meeting La June, I was struck by her quiet, gentle demeanor. Her broad smile exuded warmth and graciousness, an undeniable sign of those who are secure, confident, and at peace within. Immediately likeable, she exudes a certain air that makes you to want to know more about her. Her youthful appearance belies her many years with the W.K. Kellogg Foundation where she worked her way up to her current position of CEO.

La June spoke with the ease and conviction found in those who know they are in the right place at the right time, doing the right work for the right reasons. If you were to meet her, I am confident that you would be struck, like I was, by La June's transparency and her respect and genuine concern for people. A family and community advocate, team builder and fair-minded leader, she embodies a multitude of leadership qualities, including an unshakable belief in her goals and abilities. She epitomizes the leader who cares deeply and listens intently, qualities she values in others. This hallmark of her leadership has served her well in her tenure at the foundation, propelling her to the top as she faced some massive career challenges. Working closely with (mostly) well-intentioned men possessing little insight or understanding about one of the largest "in need" populations the foundation sought to serve, La June found a way for her rational, matter-of-fact voice to eventually rise above the discourse and be heard, for the benefit of all.

Passionate about the W.K. Kellogg mission to serve vulnerable children, she works to connect theory with practice where projected models, creative ideas, and proven practices among community partners enhance the long-term potential of children served by the foundation. She seeks to create better methods and structures for providing education, career training, and support services while increasing the efficiency and effectiveness of the organization.

La June is convinced that people work best when they understand the guidelines or rules of the game. Systems lacking rules or boundaries lead to unhealthy internal competition, causing needless stress and perpetual positioning. She is the kind of leader who sets the vision and provides parameters but gives members of the foundation a voice in setting direction and defining results. La June gives everyone the space in which to be innovative in how plans get developed. As a result, her people understand the role they play in making a difference for the populations they serve.

Pivotal Career Points

From my interview with La June, three major accomplishments stand out. The first was her willingness to persevere over the long term. Consider that as a minority female she remained in a traditional organization for nearly three decades, purposely establishing and maintaining a stellar reputation for her quality of work. Her commitment to understanding the mission, building enduring relationships, and establishing high levels of credibility and integrity all contributed to her being selected for the top leadership role.

This took determination, commitment, and dogged perseverance. As the W. K. Kellogg Foundation grew and transformed, so did she, while always continuing to support the mission. Driven by her desire to learn, grow, and take on more responsibilities over the years, this unstoppable woman continued moving on and up. Such staying power is truly an accomplishment.

One incident that La June never listed as an accomplishment, but seemed major to me, was a courageous stance she took early on in her career that firmed up her platform for the future. Finding herself unfairly distrusted and disrespected by her manager's boss who accused her of failing on a project, she persevered through the injustice instead of overreacting or resigning. She was later exonerated. Under pressure, La June had the conviction to stand up for her principles because she believed it was the right thing to do. As the CEO and leader of the foundation, she created a culture where others are encouraged to do the same.

Another accomplishment is her role in the development of the people around her. Those who have wanted to enhance their skills and develop in their positions found that La June richly contributed to their growth, helped them advance, and encouraged them to be all they could be within the organization.

Principles and Philosophy

Drawing from both her personal and professional experiences, La June Montgomery Tabron is very clear on the origins of her philosophy about life, work, philanthropy, and leadership. Here is what she shared with me:

"Being number nine in a family of ten children, I had a lot of examples to learn from. I could either follow my siblings' good behavior or bad behavior. So part of my development was shaped, not just by myself, but by the other members of my family, with all of the knowledge that those eight before me brought to the table. From there, I could then pass it on to number ten. That was the beginning of who and what shaped who I am today.

Life in my home could be chaotic at times, but we grounded ourselves in music. That was the uniting force in our house. We all came together—none of us were professional singers—but we all sang together, and that, I think, was special. Family unity was nurtured in our house, but in a very non-traditional kind of way. We sat around the table at Thanksgiving and other very important days, but we didn't sit at the table every night and have dinner together. But we had a bond. Most importantly, we came together when there was a crisis. Nothing was hidden. That's why I have a strong belief in transparency.

That's how I grew up; everything was out on the table and you could not hide anything. You were accountable to every other member of the family if something was out of sorts. So part of the family nurturing was through high expectations from every single member in the family.

One of the things that I have continued to do is to look for people who will hold me accountable. When you move away from your family you have to find people who will tell you the truth, who will expect more from you no matter what you're doing, and then give you some good advice, or at least another perspective, on how you can get there.

Why go through something if someone else has already done it and can help you figure it out? That's what learning and knowledge is all about. Because people are sometimes afraid to ask for help, as a leader, you have to find a way to give help and anticipate people asking for it even when they're not asking.

Personally, I believe that there is a greater spirit that guides us, and there are people who are meant to be in your life to help you. You have to seek those people out. Trust your gut, and then find people who can help you get there. Be true to yourself. You have to enjoy what you are doing, and I do. Part of my enjoyment is that I know that I'm serving children. As a child, I was served, and I wouldn't be where I am if I hadn't been served."

Suggestions for Your Leadership Development

In asking what La June would offer to emerging leaders, here are her thoughts and words of wisdom:

"One piece of advice—and I had to learn this myself—is to persevere. I knew in my heart what I wanted to do, and in some ways I knew that this was the right place to do it, and I couldn't allow circumstances to take from me what I felt I'd been prepared to do.

I had to stay focused because people can sometimes pull you off purpose. If I had gotten upset every time I thought there was someone I didn't feel like dealing with every day, I would have been knocked off course, and ended up being somewhere else, starting over, doing something else. But there was something deep within me that said, 'If I feel as though I'm where I'm supposed to be, maybe it's that person who needs to leave, and it's not always that I need to pull that trigger.' So knowing deeply what works for you, and staying true to your North Star and not allowing circumstances to drive you off course—persevering—would be my advice.

I find that younger people, after a year or two, move on. When I look at a resume, if I see they've had five jobs in ten years, I always want to find out why. I understand that there's a level of curiosity and there's a time when you are trying to establish your fit, but my advice would be that there is a lot of learning to be done. I'd say stay in places that might feel a little uncomfortable for a while, because how you sort through things and develop in that space could be as critical as jumping somewhere else and starting all over. I like to encourage people to be strategic and not make emotional moves in their careers."

CLOSING THOUGHTS

La June Montgomery Tabron's longevity with the W. F. Kellogg Foundation flies in the face of today's multi-layered career histories. Her comment about staying in an uncomfortable situation for a while and building skills that help you work through the issues instead of jumping ship has merit. Granted, we live and work in a mobile society, but when I think about some of the challenges and discomforts La June had to overcome, it's obvious she is the better for it.

Perseverance is related to long-term thinking. Learning to build bridges between yourself and others (rather than ignoring, retaliating, or fleeing) can result in a life-changing lesson that might just further your career. You build patience and character when you bide your time, waiting for the right moment to speak out with conviction and clarity while those around you are clamoring and competing to be heard.

Throughout her career, La June has used the passing of time to her advantage. Instead of bowing to impatience or raising cries of injustice, she made a commitment to persevere for the long term and it paid off. Not only has she achieved her dream, the far-reaching work she is supporting as CEO of the W. K. Kellogg Foundation helps fulfill dreams for vulnerable children in the United States, Mexico, Haiti, South America, and Africa who might not otherwise realize their potential.

Oprah Winfrey once said, *"What I know is, if you do work that you love, and the work fulfills you, the rest will come."* La June Tabron is living proof of this belief. The only thing she might add is, *"It will require perseverance."*

—— PROFILE ——

Cheryle Touchton

BA, University of Florida MA, Jacksonville University

Leader at a Glance

Traveling business consultant turned CEO who rescued three techy "brainiacs" and their floundering business until she found her jazz and took a surprisingly different leadership path.

Career Synopsis

Cheryle Touchton, a music major in college, began her career in a consultant role with Yamaha International. Traveling from store to store, and music school to music school, she counseled managers and storeowners on keeping their businesses profitable. From there, she returned to school for an MBA and took the helm in a tiny startup company, Pathtech Software Solutions, combining her business know-how with her skills in management and leadership.

Honors and Achievements

After 17 years of growing an organization that created and sold leading-edge software for large corporations (banks, insurance companies, hospitals, and nuclear power plants), the 80-person company Cheryle turned around from near failure to massive success, sold for $10 million. For two years, per the sales agreement, Cheryle stayed on as Vice President of Consulting Solutions for the buyer, Strategic Technologies.

Cheryle's business awards and credits include the Florida Entrepreneur of the Year, the Jacksonville Outstanding Services Business Award, and the Florida Christian Writer's Conference Outstanding Devotion Award. She has served on numerous non-profit, business, political, and religious executive boards. From there, following a strong call into the ministry, she founded Pocketful of Change Ministries, where she is in full service today as its director.

The Interview

Upon meeting Cheryle Touchton, I couldn't help but notice how she projects both a personable and businesslike aura. Meeting her at a conference, I was immediately attracted to her bold, self-assured personality. She speaks with the confidence of a woman who knows who she is, with no pretense of being otherwise. Her tall stature commands attention, but even more evident is the smooth, skillful manner in which she influences conversation.

Articulate and intentional, Cheryle is able to both hold attention and keep people engaged as she leads them down roads to new discoveries. I was captivated by how she created a safe space for interaction by her rapt attention and the subtle ways she discovered the interests of others, helping them feel understood and valued. I observed her using freshly gleaned information to steer conversations in new directions, keeping people involved and interested.

Pivotal Career Points

As CEO of Pathtech Software Solutions, Cheryle learned early on to trust her business instincts and knowledge rather than allow insecurities to rule. She had a broader view of business and understood more about running a profitable company than her three male partners who excelled in developing software, not overseeing a business. Initially, she allowed herself to be intimidated by their engineering expertise and technical skills, consenting to their right to vote on crucial issues, where they consistently voted as a bloc.

But when the company found itself in dire financial straits from poor business decisions, Cheryle mustered the courage to claim the power that was rightfully hers as CEO. Rather than calling for a vote, she declared her decision, no longer worrying about whether she'd arouse anger or be disliked. Taking charge, she made sound business decisions that protected the company's interests, knowing it was the right thing to do. And it worked.

Many of Cheryle's professional accomplishments have been driven by a strong spiritual sense of "service." In her twenties, part of that calling was in being responsible for the Yamaha music school she started, and making independent business decisions at an early age. Her music school grew to ten employees and over 500 students throughout Jacksonville. She then traveled the country as a business consultant for Yamaha International, helping other schools enjoy the same success.

With her natural ability to handle technical details and communicate with the "engineering" mind, Cheryle never shied away from a challenge, beginning with the struggling tech company founded by her husband and two engineers. When their small business landed a huge contract with the Electric Power Research Institute (beating out big companies such as General Electric), they desperately needed someone to run the business so the three engineers could concentrate on the project. That's when Cheryle moved in.

She stepped up to the plate with Pathtech Software Solutions, where she deftly guided the business, freeing up the three technical partners to create their superior products. Thanks to her business knowledge and market savvy, Cheryle championed the decision to sell their company for $10 million shortly before the Silicon Valley Tech bubble went bust, a testimony to her impressive instincts, not to mention impeccable timing!

Having gone full circle in her career, Cheryle found a way to bundle her business and people skills to gain the spiritual fulfillment she wanted and needed in her life. Today, through her on-the-road ministry, Cheryle Touchton is living her life full out, doing exactly what she feels she's been called to do. Each step of her leadership journey has prepared her for the kind of work that few can do with such grace, skill, and confidence.

She now travels the country as she did early in her career, only now evangelizing for her Pocketful of Change Ministries. Once again, she has found herself teaching managers and leaders the fundamentals of running a viable nonprofit organization.

Principles and Philosophy

You'll appreciate Cheryle's personal and professional philosophy about succeeding in whatever kind of career or vocation you choose:

"Having good communication skills is an important attribute of leadership. In the business world, I had to influence different stakeholders, not just the people reporting to me, but also customers and partners. We did a lot of lobbying in Washington DC, and I met with some of the leaders of our nation. I would have twenty minutes with them to make my case, wanting them to vote the way we needed on a particular issue. You need to present yourself well to sell your mission, and in the course of selling your mission, you have to build trust.

A good leader presents in a way that says: 'I care about you, I care about what you are doing, I care what you think and my motives are bigger than just making a profit.' In order to demonstrate all of this, what you say has to be true.

Speaking of truth, we had a situation where a project wasn't going well. I had to go to the customer and explain that we might need some more money to reach the goals, and it was our fault. We had underbid the project, and if they wanted us to accomplish what they wanted, they would need to pay more. Well, they could have easily looked at me and said, 'Well, too bad. We made a bid for this amount of money, you agreed to do it, and it is not our fault that the problem is bigger than you first anticipated.'

I really needed those people to get it; I needed them to understand that this was not something we could have foreseen, and we couldn't afford to invest in their product while losing on our side. I dealt them the truth. They had to pay us more. I sat down, looked at them, and said, 'We did the best we could do at the time; this project is something we are inventing; it has not been done before and this is what it is going to cost to finish it. We can't afford to invest in your business. Will you help us here?' And they said yes.

I cared about them and I cared about my business, and I just gave them the truth. I did this same thing when I sat down with political leaders, explaining why they needed to vote a certain way. I only lobbied where I strongly believed in the cause. I think communicating truthfully and with directness is important for leadership. It wasn't positional influence that helped me be effective; it was being able to honestly assess and champion a situation. It was being able to explain things in a truthful manner while showing that I cared. And in order to do that, I had to really care.

As for gender bias, I forgive people who think women can't do what men can do. It's never been an issue. I felt that some men (primarily older men), especially from some of the business boards I've served on, had a kind of Old Boy network, and they were just used to being together as men. They would say things that were prejudicial or that could make me feel less than one of them, and yet I was a full member of the board. So, I got over it quickly. I didn't get angry, I didn't challenge them; I didn't say, 'How dare you!' I just calmly expressed my position and they listened. I think as a female sometimes we let our anger get in the way instead of realizing that this is the way it is, and we have to deal with it."

Suggestions for Your Leadership Development

Here is what Cheryle Touchton has to say for emerging or experienced torchbearers looking to advance their careers:

"Relationships are everything, they are absolutely everything, and in order to develop a relationship you have to honestly care for the person. So, when I find myself feeling defensive or angry toward other people, feeling like I don't want to be with them, I close my mouth. I stop. I get off by myself, do some intrapersonal work, and figure out why I feel this way.

Often it is my own insecurities. Sometimes it is that I don't have myself in the right space mentally, spiritually, physically; I am not taking care of myself the way I need to. Sometimes I just need a vacation. But when I feel myself acting out of obligation and sitting there going, 'Oh gosh, I wish I didn't have to do this today,' it is always good for me to stop and pull back because relationships are critical and they have to be sincere.

Work and life balance is often an issue for us as women. I was in my beloved Jacksonville, Florida with my two children, my three grandchildren, and my elderly parents. I carved out a niche to spend time with each one of them, one-on-one. Yes, it took time away from my work. There were moments my work had to be done, and that took time away from my family. But instead of torturing myself about it, I just accepted the reality of the situation. I handled the work things I needed to handle. I handled the family things I needed and wanted to handle; I gave each of them all my best and walked away from there feeling like what I did was enough. I wish I had had this understanding early on. But at least I do now."

CLOSING THOUGHTS

Cheryle Touchton, who began her career in business, helping music store managers be more successful, has now found her niche, and this time, she is following her heart. Today Cheryle pursues her greatest spiritual calling, leaving a legacy of serving others.

I firmly believe that Cheryle represents a group of American women who are called into leadership quite unexpectedly and, because she was prepared when the door of opportunity opened, she was willing to step over the threshold. Along the way, she developed the competencies and skills required to guarantee success in whatever she endeavored.

Cheryle's business savvy, drive, and tenacity were just some of the qualities that made it possible for 79 other employees to enjoy their work and experience success as a result of her leadership. She stands as an example of the many faces of leadership in today's world, meaning that you don't need to head up a Fortune 500 company, take the helm of a prominent national non-profit, or launch an international association to be a successful leader.

What you do need is to believe in yourself, to believe in what you are doing, and to know that you can (and will) make a difference. I'm confident that Cheryle would agree with Tom Alhouse who wrote: *If you feel like giving up, give up on that feeling and give into the realization there are endless possibilities waiting to be discovered before you.*

Rather than letting leadership define you, it is completely within your realm to define what leadership means to you, but you must first believe in yourself and your vision. Who knows, you just might find a possibility for leadership in your own backyard, where and when, as the saying goes, *preparedness meets opportunity.*

PROFILE

Kathie VanderPloeg

BA, Kalamazoo College
Retired from Ship-Pac in July, 2015

Leader at a Glance

Risk taker, community minded career changer, and *internally aligned leader* whose calling shifted from the classroom to the boardroom, with a *legacy* of growing and leading the family company into the 21st Century.

Career Synopsis

Kathie VanderPloeg served as CEO and President of Ship-Pac Inc., a packaging materials company founded by her parents in 1964. With a degree in Music Education from Kalamazoo College, she could not have fathomed that one day she would run the family business. However, after working as a band director for a local school system, Kathie quickly discovered that this wasn't really a good fit and that maybe she was more suited for work in the family business.

Beginning with a position in industrial sales, over the next 25 years, she gained experience in every area of the company. By then, her parents were ready to select a second-generation successor, either Kathie or one of her brothers who also worked in the company. With fairness as his guide, their father decided that each of his three children would create their own business plan for the company, along with a strategy for securing the finances necessary for purchasing the business.

Striving for complete impartiality, he recruited independent board members to review the three proposals and gather information from the stakeholders to help him and his wife make the difficult decision as to who would be the best choice. The board recommended that Kathie be given the opportunity to buy the business.

Honors and Achievements

Under Kathie's leadership spanning 15 years, her company expanded its distribution focus to include packaging equipment systems integration, janitorial/sanitation/cleaning supplies and equipment, food packaging supplies and equipment, and safety supplies, plus equipment service and repair. Ship-Pac, recently sold to HP Products, continues as a thriving business.

Kathie's commitment to the community is evident by her service as a director of Southwest Michigan First, Partners Worldwide, World Presidents Organization (West Michigan Chapter), and Afflink. In the past, she served as a director of Southwest Michigan Healthcare Coalition, State of Michigan Certificate of Need Commission, Foundation Board of Trustees of Davenport University, Greater Kalamazoo United Way, Goodwill Industries, Kalamazoo Symphony Orchestra, and the Sacred Music Festival. Kathie has also been on the Business Advisory Council of Western Michigan University and a member of the Kalamazoo Rotary Club and Young Presidents' Organization.

The Interview

In meeting Kathie VanderPloeg, you might assess her as a conscientious businesswoman who took her role as CEO of Ship-Pac seriously. A tasteful dresser, leaning toward the classic, conservative side, I noted how she took a moment to think before answering my questions. When Kathie spoke, she did so in measured tones and with the confidence and comfort associated with authenticity. It was apparent through her responses that she is an analytical person and a deep thinker who plans for every possibility. What was even more apparent was her expansively warm heart indicating that she is a people person to the core.

In our interview, Kathie was welcoming, smiled readily, and made me feel at home instantly. She was immediately likeable. There was no pretense with this "what you see is what you get" woman. An unassuming, conscientious leader, Kathie worked tirelessly throughout her career while generously contributing to the community that provided her and her family with so much.

During our conversation, it became clear to me that Kathie deeply valued her people, and that her employees were like family to her. She knew them all, respected them, spoke highly of them, and truly cared about each of them. She never made a decision without considering its impact on her employees.

Pivotal Career Points

Kathie VanderPloeg, caring employer, levelheaded businesswoman with a strong commitment to her community and a marketplace that supported her, possessed the courage to "course correct" early in her career. Leaving the profession for which she had carefully prepared, Kathie risked disappointing those who had supported and encouraged her choice of a career in music education.

She left the classroom to follow her natural bent for business, which eventually led to her place in the boardroom, making her parents proud of the choice they had made. As the eldest of three, Kathie always felt compelled to set the bar high and prove herself, working hard to overcome the obstacles. In the late 1970's when she came into the business, there were few women in industrial sales. At that time, it was highly uncommon for a woman to take the reins in a second-generation transition. But through diligence, hard work, and passion, Kathie broke her own ground. Honing her communication skills, she shared her compelling vision and built trusting relationships with employees. Thanks to her efforts, she steered her ever-expanding company into the 21st Century.

Kathie's achievements are many and varied, but the one that stands out to me is that she had the fortitude to risk buying the family business, which meant buying her brothers' and parents' shares, which made her the sole owner of the company. This meant stripping all the profits from the business and being heavily leveraged for a number of years. But thanks to her sharp business mind, careful planning, loyal employees, and the ability to maintain a good relationship with her bank, she succeeded.

Principles and Philosophy

Every outstanding woman in this book has strong convictions about leadership and success. Here is what Kathie VanderPloeg had to say on the subject:

"I had to do a lot of soul searching before I put together a plan for running the business. I had to think long and hard about the people that were working for me. There was a strong management team, but I did not know whether that management team would stay with me once my parents had retired. It was important to find out through our board members that the stakeholders would support me. When you make a big decision, you really want to know that you can be confident going forward and that, though it may not be easy, people will stand with you.

Being in a family business is complicated because when you come into the business, you really have an uphill battle to gain credibility. You need to earn people's trust and respect; you don't get that just because you are the son or daughter of an owner. By the time I bought the company, I had already been in the business about twenty-five years. I knew our industry well, I knew our business well, and I had worked in every area of our business, with all of our employees, so it was natural to make that transition, but it was also a big step.

As a woman, this can be difficult because we might not be seen as natural successors or natural managers or leaders; and, unfortunately, as women, sometimes we are our own worst enemies. We are not necessarily supportive of each other, and so I think it is really important to find a support system. Coming into the business in the 70s, when women were not predominant, it was important to me that I gain credibility and have mentors who could help me. I developed some mentors within our customer base and within our vendor base. I see, as I am trying to mentor others today, that this is an important part of the process. And you may need to purposely seek out certain individuals to do that for you.

I learned the hard way that, as a leader, not everyone is going to like you. It was a difficult lesson for me to learn. I thought that

I could make everyone like me, and I had to learn that that is not going to happen. Leaders have to make difficult decisions, they have to do things that people don't always enjoy or don't necessarily like, and, in a lot of cases, you have an impact on people's futures. I needed to get over my need to be liked early on."

Suggestions for Your Leadership Development

Here are Kathie's thoughts and suggestions for today's emerging and developing leaders who want to advance in their careers:

"It's important to keep developing oneself continuously. I read a lot. I recognized that I not only needed to learn and to develop my skills, but also I needed to know what is going on in the world. It is shocking to me to realize how little people really listen to the news, or read a newspaper, and that there are even fewer people who will pick up any kind of book to improve themselves or to understand what is going on in business today.

Personally, I need to be continuously educating myself, including those things that have to do with the global economy and how that impacts us.

Giving back is another value that I hold most important. Giving was ingrained in me as a child. My parents felt that because our local community and marketplace was so supportive of our business, we needed to give back and my brothers and I learned how to do that from a very early age. In our business, part of our profits get set aside every year for contributing money to organizations we believe we need to be helping. We give to the community, we give to the marketplace in the areas that we are serving, and we do that on an international basis, as well.

My husband and I have been deeply involved in an organization that does micro-loan financing to a group in Kenya. We have been personally involved in raising the money to provide those loans, and in being mentors to Kenyan businesspeople who are starting their own enterprises. Now we are considering a dairy farm project in Kenya. In both cases, the goal is to alleviate poverty in their families and in communities where they can put people to work.

The most important piece of advice I would give to leaders today is to be sure that you keep contributing to the community because you aren't the only one involved in your success. It not only takes a base of employees who are supporting the organization, but it also takes a whole marketplace that is helping your business be successful. You are not in business just to create as much profit and wealth as you can for yourself, but to be able to give something of that back."

CLOSING THOUGHTS

Kathie VanderPloeg is a woman of courage, strength, and compassion. She is a woman who has always been driven by an inner compass, willing to follow her true calling even when it meant disappointing others who had a different plan for her life. She walks her talk, steeping herself in knowledge—knowledge of those for whom she is responsible as a leader, knowledge of her business, and knowledge of the world at large. She thoughtfully considers the impact of her actions before ever making a final decision. Her success speaks to the fact that she is a smart leader, anything but myopic. It's safe to say that Kathy, who looks outside herself to the larger community and always with an eye on the greater good, reveals herself as a leader who genuinely cares about others.

Kathie VanderPloeg clearly would agree with Winston Churchill who said, *"We make a living by what we get. We make a life by what we give."* May Kathie's focus on serving the larger community through her philanthropic work be an inspiration and catalyst for what and how you give. Guaranteed, your life will change, and who knows how many other lives will be altered as a result.

PART TWO

LEADERSHIP
CORNERSTONES

CORNERSTONE

CHARACTER

The Three Bs of Character:

Become

Internally Aligned

Boost

Your Bouyancy

Believe

Believe in Yourself

CHAPTER 1

CHARACTER: THE FIRST LEADERSHIP CORNERSTONE

"Character cannot be developed in ease and quiet. Only through experience of trial and suffering can the soul be strengthened, ambition inspired, and success achieved."–Helen Keller

Leaders come in many forms, from exceptional to inept and everywhere in between. You've observed leaders who finger point and blame when things go wrong and others who take full responsibility for their actions. You've seen leaders who do as little as possible while taking credit for results, and you've known some who recognize and reward good work. You've watched leaders fail to take action under pressure while others possessed the courage to make tough decisions. All of these examples are intimately related to the subject of character, or lack of it.

When I consider the full spectrum of leadership behaviors, I am convinced that a leader's true *character*—the first of The Four Cornerstones of Leadership and the one from which all other leadership qualities emanate—is most evident when the stakes are high and the pressure is on. The essence of a leader's character, however, is defined and refined with every daily decision or action the leader makes, whether operating in the presence of others or all alone. If you want an example of indomitable character, read on.

Character Personified

Her name is Pat, a self-described "fighter." Little did she know at age 59 she would be in the fight of her life with her most formidable opponent. She didn't run away in fear and hide. She didn't become bitter or angry. She didn't lose her will to win. She did what she has spent her life doing—a habit she developed as a kid growing up on a farm—she faced her opponent head on with openness and courage and the will to win.

Perhaps you've heard of Pat Summitt, head coach for the Tennessee Lady Vols and the winningest collegiate basketball coach in history. Her fiercest opponent? A diagnosis of early-onset Alzheimer's.

Shortly after her diagnosis, confronted by a litany of "can'ts", Pat had a conversation with her son Tyler, which she recounts in her book, *Sum It Up!*

> *"There was only one 'can't' I would accept regarding the illness. 'I can't change it,' I told Tyler. 'But I can try to do something about it.' I was determined to make a list of the 'cans': I can continue to work for as long as possible—I refuse to stay at home and rot away. I can resist the pressure to retire and disappear. I can decline to be afraid or self-conscious. I can try to be an example; it's easy to tell people how things are done; real teachers show people how things are done. I can joke about it. 'I've forgotten I have it,' I told Tyler. I can fight. I'd always told our players that attitude is a choice. 'It is what it is,' I said, 'but it will become what you make of it.'"* [1]

And sum it up, she did. She would lead by example. She would not give up in the face of adversity; she would not be afraid or worry about what others thought. She would continue to exemplify the mindset of a winner, a true leader. She would not give the minimum and think only of herself. She would capitalize on the time available to inspire others to stay focused on their purpose.

Summitt set a new standard for excellence and forever changed the perception of women's collegiate basketball. Since her diagnosis, she has again raised the bar on openness and courage as she looks to make a difference of an altogether different kind. In November 2011, Pat Summitt announced the formation of her foundation, the Pat Summitt Foundation Fund, with the proceeds going toward cutting edge Alzheimer's research. That same year the United States Sports Academy awarded her its 2011

Mildred "Babe" Didrikson Zaharias Courage Award for her indomitable spirit in her public battle against her debilitating disease.

Among a host of other awards and accolades, she received the 2011 Maggie Dixon Courage Award. The *Huffington Post* named Summitt a *2011 Game Changer, an innovator, leader, and role model who is changing the way we look at the world and the way we live in it.* In 2012, she was honored with the Global ATHENA Leadership Award and the Billie Jean King Legacy Award, presented by the United States Tennis Association. The list goes on.[2]

Pat Summitt has never shied from a challenge, even when it's difficult, uncomfortable, requires an abundance of energy, or puts her at risk. She believes in herself and her mission and uses every opportunity to grow, focusing continually on doing whatever is best to reach the goal. She continually works toward excellence and inspires and motivates others to do likewise, adhering to her values and never giving in to pressure to act otherwise. Pat is committed to excellence and has instilled that same desire in her players who have risen to the occasion time and again. She continues to serve as a shining exemplar of servant leadership, selfless giving, and resilience. She is someone others surely aspire to emulate.

Suffice it to say that Pat, a public figure for over forty years, is a woman of strong character—a woman whom many would describe as unstoppable, just like the twelve leaders profiled in this book. Though not as widely known as Pat, the twelve Unstoppables also possess that same strength of character. Like Pat, they are women of purpose with a deep desire to excel and help others to bring out their best. Aligned with who and what they profess to be, they are able to act in the face of fear. Adversity only makes them stronger and wiser; they are women of moral and ethical intelligence—the stuff of which unstoppable leaders are made.

Character is a Choice

In reading about Pat Summit, perhaps you've wondered about the strength of your character and how you might handle your greatest challenge in life. I did, and it's worth thinking about. Do you consistently walk your talk? Do you have a personal set of standards for yourself that you refuse to compromise? Do you adhere to a high moral code with all the people with whom you come in contact? Character and effective leadership cannot be separated; they are intrinsically connected. Our daily actions put our character on full display for others to witness (and ourselves, if we're paying attention). How people experience our leadership, the reality of what we say and do, helps them decide whether or not they trust us enough to follow our lead.

Every day, as you are undoubtedly aware, you have a chance to choose how you will respond to reality; to events large and small, difficult or easy, complex or simple. How you choose to respond ultimately determines the kind of leader you will become, forming your character in the process. The decisions you make will determine the strength of your following; for it's true that we cannot give to others what we do not possess.

As with Pat Summitt and other examples in this book, every leadership accomplishment is directly tied to the leader's character. All twelve of our unstoppable leaders demonstrate a willingness to walk their talk, a willingness to be internally controlled. As Naomi Rhode said: *"All leadership starts with* being; *the being is so much more than the* doing." In other words, who we are on the inside, our character, always shows on the outside through actions. Exceptional leadership demands strong, abiding character.

Character Defines Us, Inside and Out

If I asked you to name some of the great leaders in history, your list might include men and women of remarkable character such as Eleanor Roosevelt, Sojourner Truth, Helen Keller, Abraham Lincoln, Franklin D. Roosevelt, Winston Churchill, Margaret Thatcher, Ronald Reagan, and maybe even Malala Yousafzai (the Pakistani schoolgirl who stood up for girl's education and was shot in the head by the Taliban and survived; an activist for female education; the youngest Nobel Peace Prize recipient). Truly great leaders command authority and influence because they believe in themselves and what they stand for. They consistently adhere to principles or praiseworthy values and ethics that, for them, are non-negotiable. As a result, they are resilient in the face of challenges and even failures, destined to rise above them.

Our twelve women leaders have each faced character-defining decisions in the course of their lives. Perhaps there were times when those decisions looked unwise to others. However, through strength of character and uncompromising belief in what they held dear, these women made pivotal, perhaps sometimes unpopular, decisions, regardless of what others thought. I know from our interviews that they faced challenges, navigated change, and overcame failure because they were resilient and had the personal resolve to keep going. It may not have been easy, but the choices they made shaped their characters and allowed them to become the successful leaders they are today.

Facing the Truth

Regardless of the arena—political, academic, corporate, or religious—at some point, all leaders must look in the mirror and face the truth about themselves and their actions. This truth was never stated more clearly than in Harper Lee's 1960 Pulitzer Prize winning novel, *To Kill a Mockingbird*. Main character, lawyer Atticus Finch, simply said: *"They're certainly entitled to think that, and they're entitled to full respect for their opinions... but before I can live with other folks I've got to live with myself. The one thing that doesn't abide by majority rule is a person's conscience."* There is a correlation between one's character and one's conscience, the latter reflecting what one believes to be morally and ethically right or wrong. Living in accord with a mature conscience is what builds strong character.

Character was something our father attempted to build in my eight siblings and me while growing up. Following my father's funeral, my brother Bob found a heavily yellowed piece of paper under the glass top on Dad's desk. It was this poem, written in 1934 by Dale Wimbrow

The Guy in the Glass

When you get what you want in your struggle for pelf,
And the world makes you King for a day,
Then go to the mirror and look at yourself,
And see what that guy has to say.

For it isn't your Father, or Mother, or Wife,
Whose judgment upon you must pass.
The feller whose verdict counts most in your life
Is the guy staring back from the glass.

He's the feller to please, never mind all the rest,
For he's with you clear up to the end,
And you've passed your most dangerous, difficult test
If the guy in the glass is your friend.

You may be like Jack Horner and "chisel" a plum,
And think you're a wonderful guy,
But the man in the glass says you're only a bum
If you can't look him straight in the eye.

You can fool the whole world down that pathway of years,
And get pats on the back as you pass,
But your final reward will be heartaches and tears
If you've cheated the guy in the glass.[3]

Wimbrow understood the connection between one's character and self-respect, but he seemed a little off when he wrote, *"You can fool the whole world...."* That's not been my experience, and maybe it hasn't been yours either. You're undoubtedly familiar with the quote: *You can fool all the people some of the time and some of the people all the time, but you cannot fool all the people all the time.* It's not as easy to fool people as you might think. Or yourself.

If a leader doesn't fulfill her promises, people know it. If she pads her expense account, people know it. If a leader doesn't keep her word or if she bad-mouths those she supervises, people know it. If she invades people's privacy, or blames others to cover up her own mistakes, people know it. But most profoundly, if she is a phony, if she is faking it, or being dishonest, when she looks in the mirror, *she* knows it.

Successful leaders like the women profiled are driven by conscience and character. They know the difference between right and wrong, true and false, honest and dishonest. They live by a sense of fairness, honesty, humility, courage, respect, and contribution: their truth speaks for itself.

At the luncheon that followed my dad's funeral, members of the overflowing crowd reiterated the fact that our father was a born leader, a man of integrity who lived his life based on principles that reflected a higher standard. People knew it; they trusted him, and sought his leadership. In the end, it's safe to say that the man in the glass was my father's friend, just as it is sure to be for any leader, formal or informal, who leads by moral authority that comes from living a life of honesty, a life of integrity, a life that aligns belief and values with actions.

I regard *character* as the primary leadership cornerstone because it fundamentally drives great leadership. One may be a successful leader, but to leave a lasting legacy, a leader needs the kind of character others want to emulate. During my conversations with the twelve women selected for this book, I discovered three traits that showed up repeatedly, across the board, and they nicely complement character. These traits, running like a common theme throughout these women's lives, played an important role in their journey toward reaching the top. I invite you to determine the extent to which you possess these character traits and consider how you might cultivate them at deeper levels.

The Three *Bs* of Character:

Become internally aligned.
Boost your buoyancy.
Believe in yourself.

THE COMMON THREAD
OF CHARACTER

We all want to work with people of good character— and we know that character defies a specific definition. Ask ten different people to define character, and you get ten different descriptions. Character is complex. Most dictionaries state that character has to do with the "mental and ethical traits that mark us." We recognize the character of others by the choices they make and the behaviors they engage in, though style may differ from person to person. In this section we explore three character traits all twelve unstoppable leaders possess. While their personalities markedly differ, they share a common thread in the expression of their character: alignment with their deeply held beliefs and values; resilience in the face of setbacks, mistakes or failures, and a deep-seated belief in themselves.

CHAPTER 2

BECOME INTERNALLY ALIGNED

*"Stand up straight and realize who you are, that
you tower over your circumstances. You are a child
of God. Stand up straight." –Maya Angelou*

Internal alignment demands an adherence to values, beliefs, and moral
and ethical standards to which we hold ourselves—those things that
serve as the rules of the road for how we live life. Internally aligned
leaders have a clear knowledge and understanding of themselves, what
they believe, and what they value. They demonstrate their beliefs and values with every action they take. Though remaining internally aligned in
good times and bad may sound difficult, the women leaders in this book
have not only demonstrated it but have proven alignment to be a critical
piece to their self-fulfillment and success.

Values and Beliefs: A Driver of Alignment

In this chapter, we take a closer look at values and the beliefs we hold
concerning ourselves—those standards of behavior we passionately practice. For example, if I say I value compassion, I demonstrate it by all of
my actions, with everyone. If I say I value honesty, I am honest in all my
dealings, fulfilling promises, and honoring the dignity of others. If I should
renege on a promise, break a commitment, or be duplicitous, I am being
untrue to who I say I am and failing to be internally aligned.

When writing about internal alignment, I can't help but think about
when my daughter, Lisa, and my son, Joey, were born. I can say with all
sincerity that these were the happiest two days of my life, stirring intense
feelings of love and compassion I have never felt for another human being.
The first time I held my children in my arms, I made a silent promise to

them. I would never let them go hungry; I would die protecting them if it came to that; I would suffer whatever necessary to ensure that they had everything they needed to be healthy and happy in their lives. This commitment made me powerful as a mother. All my actions supporting my children's upbringing were powered by this conviction. Next to my husband, my children were the most important people in my life, as they were totally dependent on me. Everyone else took third place.

I can't say that I operate at that same intensity level with some other values in my life. I love my friends, but sometimes end up cancelling our dates because of work or family priorities. I value my health, but I sometimes eat food I know is not healthy, or I slip up on gym time because I feel lazy. In areas where my values are negotiable, I am not so adamant as I am in my role as a mother.

Alignment Connects with Commitment

Being true to our most important commitments makes us powerful in that aspect of our personality. For example, there is probably one person in your life that values being on time for events because she respects the fact that others are counting on her. You could set a clock by her timeliness; she's the first to show up at meetings, parties, and even casual get-togethers. Most everyone respects her consistency, though some may tease about her punctuality. Such humor is often couched in our embarrassment at not being able to have such a personal alignment with time.

Now, think of another person you know who consistently delivers on her promises. When she says she will complete a report or project at a particular date and time, you can rely on her to do so. If she says she will fill in for you at an important meeting, you know she will. There will be no call at the last minute with an excuse as to why she can't make it. Her dependability garners everybody's respect because she's someone who can be counted on. Integrity, the practice of adhering to our values in public and in private, lends potency to our actions. Lillian Bauder says, *"The most effective leader must have integrity; your word really does have to be your honor. Many leaders don't understand that integrity is absolutely critical to their effectiveness."*

Consider Mahatma Gandhi, who advocated the value of "ahimsa" (non-violence) in his fight to win independence for India. Yet, this value was not limited to his political activities. This same principle of nonviolence permeated all of his actions—in his personal life, his professional life, his teachings, and speeches. Today the value of nonviolent dissent is synonymous with Gandhi; he remains a worldwide symbol of peaceful resistance because he not only advocated those values, he lived them. As a leader he generated in his followers a belief in this value; he established non-violence as a principle of the freedom struggle he led. His power came from the fact that everybody around him—his followers, his enemies, the entire world—learned that he would not budge from his value of *ahimsa.*

Values Keep Us Aligned in Tough Times

The women I interviewed for this book also embraced and demonstrated values such as compassion, integrity, and fairness. Some leaders talk a good game, but each of these unstoppable women diligently practice the values they espouse. Perhaps there were times when they may have been momentarily tempted to make decisions that were in opposition to what they believed, but in the long run, they held fast to what they considered their non-negotiable values. Every one of them embodied the stance of *"This is who I am, and I will not apologize for it."*

Ruth Shaw remembers a moment early on in her long career—a time when she was not completely confident in a new job, and would've liked to have pulled off a do-over. She says, *"I did not have a lot of expertise in finance and I leaned on some folks in the financial area who were quite expert there. But they did not share the view I had about how one built teams, how one should treat team members with respect, and it created a block. It hindered my ability to build a team and make the kind of contribution I wanted to in that setting. I tolerated a real misalignment in values for too long."* Though she freely admits having made that mistake early in her career, she learned from it. From then on, trusting in her own values and beliefs, refusing to live by another's "rules," ultimately served her well on her path to uncommon success.

Patricia Caruso is another excellent example of a leader who realized the importance of adhering to her values. One of her strongest values is compassion, as expressed repeatedly throughout her interview. I was struck by the extent to which she was willing to stand up for that value. Patricia relates an incident when, as the director of corrections for the State of

Michigan, she had to close down several prisons due to budget cuts. One of these prisons was where she had been part of opening the prison as the business manager, and the prison's staff was very dear to her. In fact, the same week the prison's closing announcement was to be made, she had been invited as a special guest to their 20th anniversary celebration.

Patricia had the difficult task of having to break the news that the prison would be closed and that employees would lose their jobs. Being the director, Patricia could easily have delegated the dirty work to someone else, but she chose to deliver the message herself to ensure that the news was communicated with compassion. She said that when she made the announcement, she was so overcome with emotion she found herself choking up.

Patricia Caruso didn't just talk about compassion as being a value—she demonstrated it repeatedly, often in difficult circumstances. Not only did she face the music and personally deliver the bad news to prison staff, but she offered to withdraw her acceptance of their invitation to attend their 20th year anniversary celebration if they deemed it too uncomfortable for the staff to have her present. They were so taken by her courage and compassion in coming to them directly, they said that they could think of no one more appropriate to be their guest. In each of these examples, it was Patricia's character that made it possible to hold fast to her values, even under pressure. That's the kind of consistency and integrity it takes to be a strong leader.

Values Keep Us Focused on Doing the Right Thing

One of the core values of La June Tabron is standing up for what she believes is right. During her long career at the Kellogg Foundation, La June has experienced many opportunities to demonstrate her commitment to this value. In one incident, her boss's boss came down hard on her to deliver a project with a very tight deadline, which involved implementation of a major system change over which La June was responsible but had had no input. La June was preemptively accused of failing on the project prior to the deadline as her boss didn't feel she could possibly complete the project on time.

La June expressed her indignation to her mentor and told him that she had decided to quit in protest to such unfairness, but only after she completed the project on time and with 100 percent accuracy. Taking her mentor's advice, she decided not to quit and persevered through the injustice, delivering the project on time and with complete accuracy, proving the accusation both unjust and erroneous.

Years later when she became the CEO of the organization, one of the first things she did was to initiate a culture change, making it easier for people to speak up about issues or question the status quo to ultimately benefit those served by the organization. She lives her value of doing the right thing, and has established it as a valued principle at the Foundation.

All twelve unstoppable leaders seem to have found their personal *North Star* and remained true to it, regardless of the challenges they faced. They found opportunities to live their values, inculcating those values in the people they influenced: team members, colleagues, clients, and even communities. These leaders are internally aligned from belief to action.

I have spoken on the subject of internal alignment in many of my speaking engagements, referring to leaders who adhere to their principles, values, or standards of behavior as "aligned leaders." For this reason, my organization's name is *The Aligned Leader Institute*. Aligned leaders, in my experience, commit to living life in accordance with what they value. If aligned leaders value honesty and openness, they live their truth, no matter how difficult. They admit to mistakes and acknowledge shortcomings. If they say they value integrity, they are ethical in their dealings, even when it doesn't serve them.

If they live by the principle of lifelong learning, that they hunger for what feeds them, they surround themselves with books and resources that nourish, inspire, and propel them. If they live by the universal law of sowing and reaping, they cultivate quality relationships; both they and their organizations reap the rewards of mutual respect and caring. If they live by the principle of servant leadership, they never ask people to do what they themselves are not willing to do. They lead by example. In short, servant leaders say and do the things that align them with what they hold most important. Inwardly, they may not feel respectful of others at all times, but they always treat others with esteem. They might be tempted to cross the ethics line, but they don't. They may not feel like forgiving, but they do. In other words, they live what Martha Mertz calls *living authentically*.

Authentic Living Brings Harmony

In her interview, Martha says, *"If people aren't living what they say they believe, then they're not in harmony with themselves. Those who are not in harmony with themselves are not going to be able to inspire others to follow after them. So in my efforts to keep in harmony, I try to make sure that the values that I believe in are reflected in what I am doing every day."*

As a leader, being internally aligned, authentic, and true to who you are, imbues you with credibility. When people see that their leader stands by what she claims to believe in, regardless of the circumstance, they know the leader is not driven by short-term, feel good or egocentric motives. This creates trust and confidence and inspires those she seeks to influence. A great leader is someone who inspires people with a compelling, worthwhile vision and then moves toward that vision in such a way that others trust that she will take them there.

A leader's consistency of thought and action is at the heart of people's willingness to set aside their own agendas and take up the leader's vision. People have to believe that, as a leader, you are what and who you say you are, and that you will deliver on what you promise. They have to believe that, as their leader, you will have their best interests at heart. They have to believe you are a person of truth and that you practice what you preach, every day in every action you take, big or small. They have to believe you will do the right thing in the right way for the right reason.

Dr. Lillian Bauder exemplified alignment of action with belief while CEO at Cranbrook Educational Community. Dr. Bauder had been made aware that some of the pre-school teachers were drawing bagels in front of the Jewish applicants' names. She asked the teachers the significance of the bagels. They responded that they were identifying Jewish students to make sure that those students were evenly spread throughout the school, with no heavy concentration of Jews in any one grade.

Lillian dug more deeply; she discovered a different story. The students with bagels by their names were far less likely to be admitted to the school. Once she made the discovery, she decided not to renew those particular teachers' contracts. She commented that she would like to have released them immediately, but because they were teaching younger grades, she thought it would be too disruptive to the students, so she decided not to renew their contracts for the following year.

When her intent became known to others, some of the faculty and alumni were very much opposed to it. They said, *"You're revealing our dirt in the public."* Some of the parents were opposed to it. A member of the founding family came to her and said, *"We have a six percent Jewish quota."*

Lillian, a champion of social justice, took her position to the board of trustees and said, *"If you do not want me to do this, then this job is not a good fit for me. It's not who I am; it's not what I believe. It is not what I think Cranbrook believes either."*

The board supported her; the faculty who drew the bagels departed. Lillian said that that act of standing up for her personal values was truly a *"watershed event for Cranbrook."* Today Cranbrook is an incredibly diverse, exciting community for people of all backgrounds as long as they are willing to struggle toward excellence. Lillian walked her talk, resulting in significant change.

Being internally aligned is so important to leaders that when their actions are incongruent with their espoused values, they suffer dissonance. I experienced this when writing *The Unstoppables.* My vision was to complete this project within three years, and when that didn't happen, I began waking up at night with the gnawing sensation of something left undone. Alignment is an outgrowth of character. It's about possessing the courage, discipline, and fortitude to fulfill a promise; to do what we said we would do, even if the promise is only to ourselves.

Comfort with Oneself: Another Form of Alignment

Another aspect of character that relates directly to internal alignment is being comfortable with yourself, whether it be with your gender, race, beliefs, or values. It means resisting the temptation to be overly self-critical or judging yourself harshly. It means acknowledging that you may not be perfect, but that what and who you are is absolutely good enough. It means encouraging yourself so you avoid second-guessing your actions, particularly those which intuitively seem like *the right thing to do.* For example, if you say, *"I am compassionate,"* then you want to act consistently on that value rather than being embarrassed by appearing "soft" to others. Only then will you be able to boldly live life in accordance with that value; only then will you be powerful as a compassionate leader.

Family friend, Cynthia Williams, Executive Director of Michigan Education Special Services Association, wisely says, *"People shouldn't think that when they step into a role they have to be the kind of leader they have observed, or even the kind of leader that they have admired. They have to be the kind of leader that best takes advantage of their own skills; they have to develop their own leadership style—find their own stride—and find a way to be comfortable in their own way, so that they can be the most effective individual in that role."*

Dr. Ruth Shaw discovered the importance of being comfortable with her authentic self while still in her twenties. As you learned from her profile, when applying for the position of Academic Vice President at the Dallas County Community College District, Ruth's well-meaning friends and associates felt that she needed to look older for her interview with Bill Priest, the college Chancellor, so as to appear more experienced. She bowed to their advice and dressed frumpily, pinned down all her wild beautiful hair in a bun and even carried an umbrella!

At the end of the successful interview, Priest looked her up and down and said, *"Tell me, do you always dress that way?"* Ruth responded, *"Well, no, as a matter of fact, I don't."* Priest said, *"Well, you never need do it again on my account."* Ruth goes on to say that it was a wonderful lesson about being herself. Despite dressing like an older woman, Ruth could not hide her true self, nor could she hide her intelligence and her readiness for the job as it shone through all her words and actions. She now advocates to all the women leaders she mentors the importance of being oneself.

Another aspect of aligned leadership for women is being true to one's gender and personality style, while being open to learning and self-development. Research shows that men and women are wired differently in how they think, what they value, how they communicate and interact with peers. This doesn't mean that either gender makes a superior leader. It just means that men and women have different intrinsic strengths, collectively and individually. We've come a long way from the day when "male" leadership was considered superior, though even today many women in the corporate world are battling stereotypes and prejudices that assume that female leaders should act more like their male counterparts. It helps to consider that many of the women leaders I interviewed grew up during the first waves of the feminist movement where women were expected to act more like men, yet each of them remained true to her identity as a woman.

Lillian Bauder spoke of this at length when she described a financial crisis at Cranbrook that she resolved with the help of F. Alan Smith of General Motors and Robert J. Vlasic of Vlasic Pickles and Vlasic Foods. Following the successful conclusion of this predicament, she sent the two men flowers and a bottle of champagne to express her gratitude. The men were surprised and delighted with these gifts because no one had ever done anything like that before. This was because the professional world was still dominated by male leaders, and men didn't (and still don't) typically do things like that. She said, *"Giving these gifts is really who I am. I didn't have a problem doing it, as many women who were "first women" did. Some were instead trying to be more like men so they would be more acceptable. I am always happy and comfortable being who I am."* Lillian understands her own personality, and she made the decision that she was going to lead in a way that was aligned with the woman she is.

Similarly, Cheryle Touchton speaks about a conversation she had with her father as she was repairing the old school bus she drove in her job as a sales consultant for a music company early in her career. She remembers being up to her elbows in grease as her father walked by. She looked at him and said, *"Daddy, why didn't you teach me how to work on these kinds of things?"* Her father just shook his head and said, *"Because I thought you were going to be a girl!"*

Cheryle had to battle social stereotypes to do what she loved doing—business. Like our other women leaders, Cheryle never tried to be someone she was not, and that included trying to be anything other than who she was. She said, *"I do not try to be a man. I think my strengths are wonderful in the workplace, and I think that it is useful to the corporations."* She struck a fine balance between harnessing her unique strengths as a woman leader and, at the same time, not being limited to the rigid roles that women are expected to handle.

In establishing the ATHENA Awards for women leaders, Martha Mertz, too, started with the fundamental belief that female leaders are different than male leaders—that women have their own strengths that need to be celebrated and valued. She said, *"We must no longer have what I call the 'male model' of leadership, which is more about command and control. That isn't the kind of leadership we need fifty years from now or even tomorrow. What we need now are the quiet strengths we have found in the leaders who have become ATHENA recipients."*

All of the women profiled in this book joyfully embrace and align themselves with their femininity. They celebrate their strengths as females, comfortable in the knowledge that they bring something to the table their male colleagues do not. Embracing and applying your feminine characteristics and behaviors is not about accepting the traditional stereotypes about what constitutes a woman. It is about developing a true understanding of your own innate strengths and character, knowing you don't have to emulate male styles of leadership to be effective.

Litmus Test for Determining Your Values

Sometimes people ask how a person achieves internal alignment. It's not an innate process that occurs naturally; it's something we consciously initiate and create, requiring self-assessment and reflection. Jim Rohn said, *"Character isn't something you were born with and can't change, like your fingerprints. It's something for which you must take responsibility in forming."* [4] Alignment isn't something that can be bestowed upon us, but rather it's something we cultivate over the course of our lifetime, through every experience and every decision we make.

Former President Ronald Reagan spoke clearly about how character (or alignment) gets developed when he said, *"The character that takes command in moments of crucial choices has already been determined. It has been determined by a thousand other choices made earlier, in seemingly unimportant moments. It has been determined by all the little choices of years past, by all those times when the voice of conscience was at war with the voice of temptation whispering the lie that it really doesn't matter. It has been determined by all the day-to-day decisions made when life seemed easy and crises seemed far away...the decisions that, piece by piece, bit by bit, developed habits of discipline or of laziness, habits of self-sacrifice or self-indulgence, habits of duty and honor and integrity—or dishonor and shame."* [5]

Character is built by keeping your personal values at the core of everything you do. For each one of us, personal alignment comes from deep within. After all, if we can't trust ourselves to do what we say we'll do, how can we expect others to trust us when they will be affected by decisions we make? Trust building begins by being honest with yourself. And then ensuring that every decision you make, every message you convey, everything you choose to model for others is consistently in alignment with who you are and what you truly believe in. The formation of a strong, admirable character has its roots in such alignment. This is what will make an individual a powerful leader and role model and compel others to buy into the leader's vision.

To develop a sense of genuine alignment, become intimately aware of your inner thoughts and feelings and the beliefs that drive them. By heightening your self-awareness and spending time in concerted reflection, you will be able to identify what is important to you and what is not; what you are comfortable with, and what doesn't fit; what is authentic to you and what rings false. When your behaviors are aligned with your core values, it makes responding from an authentic place an easy choice—the only choice.

If you're at all unclear as to your core values, the following personal story can provide you some insight as to how you might go about discovering them.

It was the holiday season and for the first time I took my three-year old daughter, Lisa, Christmas shopping at the local mall. The cacophony created by the hordes of shoppers, the sound of mechanical toy displays, and the buzz around special holiday retail booths made conversation difficult at best.

We were in Steketee's Department Store where I had been rifling through a rack of blouses with Lisa at my side. Seconds later I looked down to say something to her, only to discover she was gone. *"NO!"* my mind screamed as my heart raced and I charged up the stairs to find the woman staffing the PA system, all the while frantically searching the store for my little girl.

Not only did the woman on the PA show little concern, she was slow to respond, and asked too many questions. For me, there was not a moment to waste. My daughter had to be found *now*. Dashing through the store, propriety aside, I began screaming her name. *"Lisa! Lisa!"* I wailed, over and over in my desperate search. In retrospect, I must have looked like a mad woman to unsuspecting shoppers as I raced around in my frenzy.

126

But as in childbirth, it didn't matter who saw or heard me. Nothing was more important than finding my daughter.

Suddenly, two women hurried toward me, *"Have you lost a little girl?"* Wasn't it obvious!

"Yes, her name is Lisa. She's wearing a little red coat, blue corduroy pants, and Mickey Mouse boots." My words tumbled out.

"We found her in the middle of the mall, crying. She wouldn't come with us because she said that her mommy told her never to go with strangers, but she was willing to wait at one of the kiosks. Come with us, and we'll take you to her."

From a distance I could see Lisa sitting on the counter of the booth, looking scared and tearful. When our eyes met, we dissolved into sobs of relief. Upon reaching the booth, our arms flung around one another and we hung on for dear life. At that moment nothing else mattered. It was crystal clear that my family held top priority, what I valued above all else.

Years have passed. Lisa now has her own daughter, and with time, some of my values have changed, but the lesson remains as if cut in stone. If you are ever in doubt or wonder about what you value, the litmus test never changes. Your values can become clear by examining what you chase, the tenacity with which you pursue it, and the joy it brings you.

Being internally aligned with who you are and what you value breeds authenticity, a powerful leadership trait critical to building trust and credibility. It is essential to being a leader who achieves uncommon success, to being the kind of leader others wish to emulate.

As Mahatma Ghandi said, *"Your beliefs become your thoughts. Your thoughts become your words. Your words become your actions. Your actions become your habits. Your habits become your values. Your values become your destiny."* If that isn't a description of how character is formed, I don't know what is.

CHAPTER 3

BOOST YOUR BUOYANCY

"The difference between successful people and others is how long they spend time feeling sorry for themselves." –Barbara Corcoran

When my dad was in his early forties and already the father of nine children, he became seriously ill and was unable to work for two years. Our family's sole breadwinner, he was able to keep a roof over our heads and food on the table by selling off property he'd bought with money from the family farm sale. By the time my father's health was restored, there was no more land to sell, and he had to decide how to care for his sizable family. Having witnessed his parents' home burned to the ground without a lick of insurance coverage, he made the decision to start an insurance agency. With a substantial loan from a man who trusted my father to repay the money within an agreed upon period of time, my dad launched his independent insurance agency out of a small bedroom in our 1,200 square-foot home.

Within twenty years, my dad, with the help of my mother working as his full-time office manager, had repaid his loan. All nine of their children had completed their college education, and my parents were able to retire in Green Valley, Arizona, where they lived for over twenty years.

Unstoppable Leaders Bounce Back from Failure

Buoyancy—the ability to bounce back from failure—was one of my father's finest assets, and it is a characteristic of every great leader: from Abraham Lincoln to Thomas Edison; from Henry Ford to Steve Jobs; from British Prime Minister Margaret Thatcher to American Publisher Katherine Graham. There is something about one's capacity to experience setback and not be discouraged, to experience failure and yet rise above it with courage and purpose. Regardless of the obstacles they face, exceptional leaders rebound unscathed and more determined than ever. Buoyancy carries with it a staying power that attracts people, opportunities, and the resources needed to carry out one's resolve. It is the hallmark of those who succeed, of leaders who remain unstoppable and achieve uncommon success.

Consider Margaret Thatcher, the first female prime minister of Europe and the longest-serving British prime minister of the 20th century, elected for three consecutive terms. Thatcher overcame personal obstacles as well as political hurdles, including doubt and criticism from those within her own party. It is a well-known fact that Margaret Thatcher's voice undermined her image early in her career. But through diligent work with a professional voice coach, she altered her naturally strident tone—something that alienated her male colleagues—to a more commanding contralto. Margaret Thatcher was a woman who handled personal obstacles the same way she approached political challenges, head on; facing them with uncompromising determination. Throughout her tenure in office, she adhered to a strict set of principles that governed her actions and decisions, and earned her the title as Britain's Iron Lady. She truly was a giant in her time.

Effective leaders are buoyant. Those who are unable to overcome obstacles or recover from failures drastically limit their potential. Just think about it: when we are unable to reframe failures as "opportunities to learn what doesn't work," or unwilling to consider failures as "stepping stones to success," we relinquish our autonomy and personal power. If we lack the resilience to regroup after a disaster, we may find ourselves living that life of quiet desperation Henry David Thoreau described in *Civil Disobedience and other Essays*.

On the other hand, if we are able to take failure in stride and conquer the obstacles standing in the way of our goals, learning how to make decisions based on reality rather than fear, we reaffirm who we are and what we stand for. By accepting *what is* (in comparison to what we wish) and taking positive, proactive steps that drive us forward, we rebound; we bounce back even better than before.

Resilient leaders profit from all their experiences, both good and bad, and use what they learn to move toward their desired vision. The greatest and most successful leaders know they can learn from every experience.

The lessons gleaned make them stronger and wiser, and often more compassionate and forgiving. The true test of your buoyancy as a leader will always surface when you come face to face with your biggest obstacles or greatest failures. Your character is being forged every time you face a fear, surmount an obstacle, and use your worthy lessons to propel you forward.

One of my clients, Denise Crawford, CEO of the Family Health Center of Kalamazoo, Michigan, says, *"It was all of my failures and my ability to rise above those failures that strengthened my determination and resolve, knowing that I could do it. It wasn't just all of my successes, because successes often don't come with the same lesson, the same determination, the same tears, the same emotions. I actually have a plaque that sums it up well. Though quite simple, it is extremely powerful, and I have used it throughout my entire life. It simply says: 'Never, never, never give up.'"*

Ariana Huffington, Editor and Chief of the Huffington Post, said, *"We need to accept that we won't always make the right decisions, that we'll screw up royally sometimes—understanding that failure is not the opposite of success, it's part of success."* Not all of us realize that the key to success lies in failures. Yet each of us learned to walk by first falling down and getting back up, time and time again. Perhaps we are our most resilient in the first year of our lives. Maybe this is a lesson we could carry in our hearts.

In her book, *The Price of Privilege: How Parental Pressure and Material Advantage Are Creating a Generation of Disconnected and Unhappy Kids,* [6] Madeline Levine, psychologist, argues that affluent parents often shield their children from the experience of failure early in life. Parents who protect their children from struggling with setbacks inadvertently set them up for failure in adulthood because they never learned how to handle life's setbacks. Instead of over-indulging their children by fulfilling their every wish and desire, Levine believes that parents need to be focused on building life skills that allow their children to be more adaptable and resilient to challenge or hardship.

Exceptional Leaders Course Correct Quickly

The women leaders I interviewed have had their share of failures in life, and they learned from those failures. Gail McGovern expressed it beautifully when she said, *"I always tell people that they need to be resilient, which sounds simple, but is hard. You absolutely will make mistakes; it is how quickly you recover and course-correct that makes you a great leader, not the number of mistakes you make. If great leaders stick to their guns, it becomes their downfall if they don't course-correct. Instead, be resilient, and if you make a mistake, course-correct quickly."*

Gail McGovern's first ten years of her career at AT&T were riddled with setbacks and dead ends. She moved from one role to another, muddling along, as she calls it, because she never had a mentor or career guide who could advise her on career decisions. At one point, she found herself the oldest division manager in the organization; that's when she realized she had pigeon-holed herself into a mediocre career path. It was through this failure that Gail learned her lesson and forged her resiliency by making a decision that led her to a pathway of growth.

Buoyancy Involves Being Passionately True to One's Self

Lillian Bauder confided in her interview that her parents did not support her goals. They were opposed to her going to college. Later on they were opposed to her becoming a dean, and these weren't the only instances. Her parents didn't think that stepping out and becoming a leader was proper for a woman. But Lillian had been thrust into leadership positions at a young age, and she simply didn't allow her parents' attitudes to crush her resolve. Lillian refused to consider that she couldn't or shouldn't follow her passion.

My friend, Joy Strand, CEO of The McCready Foundation Health System in Crisfield, Maryland, displayed this same attitude of not allowing an unsupportive family to block her dreams of receiving an education. Joy's family spurned the idea of higher education. None of her family members on either parental side had ever received a college degree. Joy, on the other hand, was keen on going to college and secretly applied to the college of her choice. Imagine her joy when she received the acceptance letter; it was a truly great moment for her.

Unable to contain her excitement, she showed the letter to her parents, expecting them to be as overjoyed as she was. It didn't happen. She remembers her father reading the letter and then saying, *"I am not going to send you to college to find a husband."* Joy was devastated. She was seventeen years old at the time, unable to support herself through college. Shattered but determined, she didn't give up. Faced with this setback, Joy ratcheted up her resilience and resolved to hang onto her dream. And bounce back she did. At age twenty-three, Joy decided to try again, working full-time night shifts while completing her bachelor's degree. Believing that *"where there's a will, there's a way,"* Joy possessed the will and she found the way. Joy steadfastly refused to allow an early setback to define her.

Life deals each of us our share of challenges, and one of the critical characteristics distinguishing leaders who reach the highest levels of their organizations from the rest is their ability to turn stumbling blocks into stepping stones. Our women leaders faced failures, fears, and substantial challenges that could have stopped them in their tracks. But each of them, in her own way, was resilient because she was internally aligned. Every one of these leaders found a way not to just survive, but to ultimately thrive. That is buoyancy.

When faced with the curve balls life threw at our leaders, it was their wisdom, adaptability, and resilience that saw them through to greater success. In taking a moment to personalize these principles, you and I both know this to be true. We have each faced our own curve balls and learned mighty lessons from our experiences, good and bad. And when we were aligned with our true selves, deep down we knew which path to take, regardless of the difficulty level. We got up after our fall, regrouped, and resurfaced.

Simply put, success is intimately related to being passionately true to one's self and doggedly maintaining perspective. Every now and then it helps to look back on where you've been and the challenges you've faced, overcome, moved beyond, or bounced back from to get you where you are today. Take heart; this gives you a hint of the potential you possess as a leader.

Now and then I reflect on the sobering struggles my former husband and I faced in trying to launch a retail business with the deck of Michigan's economic cards stacked against us. That period of loss and hardship was decades ago, yet each decade since has presented its own series of dilemmas and decisions: starting over in a scaled down home; launching my business as a speaker and consultant; living through a divorce; dealing with two rebellious teens; getting remarried and watching my new husband lose his job, complete law school, and open up a practice at an age where most people are preparing for retirement; caregiving my parents for over half a decade until their deaths just a year apart; and last, the loss of investments in 2008 when the stock market plunged. These are the highlights of my lows, and from them I learned an enormous number of insights about my life, my values, and my passions.

Regardless of your age or stage of life you have a list of your own conquered challenges and confrontations. In my own journey, each time I faced a challenge, I chose to perceive it as an opportunity to refine who I was and remain aligned with what I valued. These are our defining moments—the times we either slink away from the adversity or step up to the plate. These are the moments where we distinguish and demonstrate leadership in the personal realm. Through my ordeals, I recognized I had the choice of either giving up or moving on, and each time I promised myself that quitting was not an option. For me, rallying and recouping was critical for not just getting my life back on track, but modeling for my children the importance of resiliency and buoyancy in times of trouble or transition.

Buoyant Leaders Look for the Lesson

When faced with setbacks, an aligned leader goes deep inside, looks for the lesson from each defining moment, and moves forward. Less hardy individuals may choose to give in or give up. Buoyancy, the ability to regroup and recover from defeat, is rooted in personal alignment, your *North Star*, your pivotal point, your inner beacon. Buoyant leaders remain patient in times of chaos or crisis and are not intimidated at the prospect of making a mistake. Their commitment triggers determination instead of defeat, fueling the ability and willingness to carefully analyze circumstances, seek feedback, and learn from mistakes. Buoyant leaders do their deep inner work and take time out to ask themselves important questions concerning the circumstances they face.

Mary Ellen Rodgers puts it well when she says, *"Don't come in with preconceived notions in terms of what is possible and what is not possible. Take time every year to sit down and ask yourself: What have I learned? How am I better? What are the things that I still need to learn? How do I put myself in a position of not being stagnant, but truly growing in ways that are important to me?"*

133

If one is internally misaligned, it would be difficult to move forward in the journey toward successful leadership, for alignment ignites resilience, the ability to recover from hardship and failure. And then there's buoyancy, which some might think of as resilience "on steroids." Where does buoyancy come from? How can one develop robust resilience in the face of failure or crisis? From my interviews with the twelve unstoppable women leaders who achieved uncommon success, it became clear that there exists an element of character that has allowed these women to bounce back from difficulties that others may have walked away from—a strong belief in one's self.

CHAPTER 4

BELIEVE IN YOURSELF

*"Aerodynamically the bumblebee shouldn't be
able to fly, but the bumblebee doesn't know that
so it goes on flying anyway." –Mary Kay Ash*

Some of the most successful leaders, particularly those who emerged from deprivation and adversity, possess and nourish a deep-seated belief and confidence in their ability to endure and flourish despite failure or hardship. Consider Oprah Winfrey, who survived childhood poverty and sexual abuse to host her award-winning *The Oprah Winfrey Show* and rise to be the world's richest, most famous and influential black woman. Add Nelson Mandela, the South African anti-apartheid revolutionary who, after twenty-seven years of imprisonment, became South Africa's first black president, elected in a fully representative democratic election in 1994. Mandela dismantled the tyranny of apartheid and fostered racial reconciliation in South Africa. Then there's Mother Theresa, 1979 Nobel Peace Prize winner and Roman Catholic Religious Sister and missionary, who spent most of her life in the slums of India providing free services to India's poorest of the poor through the Missionaries of Charity, which she established in 1950.

Let us now acknowledge that there are many leaders, unsung and unknown, who have been highly successful in their careers, and who have made significant differences in society or the organizations in which they work. We all have high achieving leaders in our own communities who serve as role models for each of us, people who grow companies, launch nonprofits, or those who challenge the status quo. For example, Dr. Patricia Numann, the first female president of the American Board of Surgery and president of the American College of Surgeons, came from a background of poverty and family illness. Her father lost his job when she was four years old and suffered a stroke when Patricia was eight, forcing her mother to become the main wage earner in the family. Despite her early hardships, Dr. Numann earned a pre-med degree, and fought entry into the surgical field, which at that time did not accept women.

She has since earned many firsts in her career: the first female surgeon and then medical director at Upstate Medical University, and vice president of the American College of Surgeons. Dr. Numann was the first woman to serve on the American Medical Association's Council on Scientific Affairs and the first female chair of the American Board of Surgery. Such success on her part stems from a family that prized excellence and hard work, as well as a lasting belief in her abilities and the confidence that she had what it took to succeed in the traditionally male-dominated field of surgery.[7]

Belief in One's Self is Nurtured in Many Ways

The leaders highlighted in this book displayed a similar confidence in themselves along with a tenacious belief in their capabilities. When Ruth Shaw moved from an academic environment to the corporate world, she knew she was taking one of the biggest risks in her career. It was only her self-confidence and faith in her ability to learn what she needed to know that allowed her to become such a phenomenal success at Duke Energy. She says, *"The single biggest thing that allowed me to succeed was the sense that 'I could do this' almost regardless of the setting. I just had a sense that I could learn and, with the help and collaboration of other people, be successful in the settings in which I found myself."*

Believing in yourself is fundamental to leadership. Unless you believe in yourself and your goals, and have the faith and confidence that you will succeed, you will be unable to translate your vision into reality. Belief in yourself and your potential is a critical first step in your leadership journey. Mary Ellen Rodgers says, *"If you are comfortable with the decisions you are making, with what you are representing, and with what you believe in, it becomes much easier to lead with conviction. That, I would say, is number one."*

For some of the women I interviewed, this confidence emanated from their acquired competence, from learning everything they could about the nature of their company; and for others, it was a faith in their capacity to learn. Kathie VanderPloeg was both confident and competent in handling the ever-expanding family business. This self-belief was a result of the knowledge and experience she gained over twenty-five years of learning the many aspects of their business.

During those years, Kathie worked in every area of the company, learning from her seniors, taking counsel from mentors, and making sure that she was completely knowledgeable and competent every step of the way. When the time came for her to throw her hat in the ring to determine who would eventually serve at the helm of Ship-Pac Inc., she was infinitely prepared to create the winning business plan. With knowledge that stretched both broad and deep, Kathie demonstrated to her parents that she was more capable than anyone else in the family to own the business and take it forward.

Cheryle Touchton developed confidence as a leader by claiming the right that was hers as CEO. Cheryle knew she had a broader view of business and understood more about running a profitable company than her three male partners, but she let herself be intimidated by their brilliant engineering minds. Cheryl consented to their right to vote on critical issues, and because they voted as a bloc, she was, in effect, silenced and her decisions nullified. Only after the company slid into dire financial straits due to poor business choices did Cheryle muster the courage to assert her rightful power. Once she began making crucial business decisions without asking for a vote from her business partners, their company regained a strong financial footing. Cheryle's desire to do the right thing won out over her need to be liked. In the process, her confidence soared and the business flourished.

Ruth Shaw's self-confidence was rooted in an unquenchable desire and ability to learn. She says, *"That period of incompetence you experience when you do not know the rules, and you think everyone else does, has never been pleasant for me. However, I've always been one to think that I can learn; that I can understand the rules of this setting and what the norms are. I can make a contribution."*

For some leaders, belief in oneself comes through a process of growth and enlightenment, of learning who they are as human beings, and discovering through experience how expansive their talents and capabilities are. For example, Pastor Beth Jones was initially tentative about taking a leadership position, not because she didn't know that leadership skills were within her, but because women were not easily received or welcomed into leadership roles in the church—especially in pulpit or lead roles. But as she grew into the role, she learned to trust herself and let the results speak for themselves. Beth says, *"I felt strongly that the Lord wanted me to focus on leading, preaching, and teaching in the church and writing books for the church. I just had to overcome the opposition I received from well-meaning people who didn't think it was right for me to take on traditional male positions. Eventually, like other women before me, I embraced my leadership responsibilities."*

For other leaders, their strong sense of self came from a nurturing and encouraging childhood environment. Denise Crawford, CEO of the Family Health Center of Kalamazoo, attributes her self-confidence to her loving and supportive mother who taught Denise to believe in herself. Naomi Rhode talks about the ongoing encouragement she received from her father.

Whenever Naomi would face a new or challenging experience, her father would remind her that she was cherished, loved, and respected by her family. Naomi recounts an incident when, around the age of twelve, she returned from camp having met a boy she was determined to marry one day. Upon telling her father about her decision, instead of his being aghast at her announcement or making fun of her childish fantasy, her father simply said, *"Wow, he must be a wonderful young man. I say that because you always make good choices, and then you always make your choices good."* The messages she received from her father allowed Naomi to internalize them and to have faith in her choices for her entire life. Interestingly, a number of years later, Naomi did marry that boy and they have had a very successful and loving marriage that spans many decades.

Naomi was also encouraged to believe in herself by a grade school teacher. Shortly before going into the 5th grade, her family moved from Fargo, North Dakota to St. Paul, Minnesota. Naomi told me that she was tall for her age, didn't know anyone, and was timid about how to break into the class of students who all knew each other. During the first recess, Naomi stayed in the cloak closet, and her 5th grade teacher, Miss Hand, found her here. She said to Naomi, *"I am so glad you are in my 5th grade class because I can tell you are a leader!"* Naomi excitedly told her that she had been the president of her 4th grade class in Fargo. Miss Hand responded with, *"Why don't you run for president of our class? You would be great with all that experience!"* Naomi said, *"Sure."* Miss Hand then said, *"The voters are out on the playground; you need to go and get to know them."* She did! She became the class president, and from then on she was on a roll. As she said, *"Leadership became the norm for me."*

Drawing from my own experience, I learned how the power of someone else's belief in you ends up fueling belief in yourself. When my father turned eighty, my eight siblings and I decided to give him a surprise party. As part of our father's birthday surprise, we created a *Story of Dad's Life* video, using photographs taken during his lifetime, including music to accompany each decade. At the end of the video, we each added our own individual footage in which we shared with our father the impact he had made on our lives.

Each clip was heartfelt; some were funny, some tongue in cheek. But my brother Pat's comments were unforgettable. Looking directly into the camera, Pat said, *"Hi Dad. As you recall, when I was ten years old, I played little league baseball, and you'd come to every game and sit in the bleachers in a spot where you could see and hear everything that went on in the dugout. Our team had a pitcher with a wicked fastball, and all the kids were afraid to catch for him. During one game, the pitcher threw one of his famous fireballs, injuring the catcher who was taken out of the game. The coach ran to the dugout and shouted, 'Hey fellas, who wants to catch?' And Dad, before anybody could say anything, you yelled from the bleachers, 'Pat'll do it; he's not afraid of anything.'*

Well, Dad, those words have stuck with me my entire life. When I was sloshing through the rice paddies in Viet Nam with a platoon following me, I was scared, but your words rang in my ears, 'Pat'll do it; he's not afraid of anything.' Your words got me through. Then, when I left the service and went to law school, that first year I was afraid I might not have what it took to make it through, but your words continued to ring in my ears, 'Pat'll do it; he's not afraid of anything.' And even today when I'm facing a tough judge in court and my case ain't all that great, your voice still rings clear, 'Pat'll do it; he's not afraid of anything.'

Dad, those words have helped me though every major fear I've ever experienced. I might be afraid, but I know that I'll get through it. I cannot tell you how grateful I am, Dad, for those few simple words, 'Pat'll do it; he's not afraid of anything.' Your words have made all the difference in my life. Thanks, Dad. I love ya. Happy 80th birthday."

My brother Pat has been wildly successful in his life and career, and he credits his success to those eight little words spoken to him when he was ten years old. Dad's words generated a deep and lasting belief in Pat's ability to work through and conquer whatever fear he was facing so he could move closer to his goals.

Regardless of where the belief in one's self takes root, this unshakeable faith has allowed our leaders to take risks and step into arenas and unknown territory where they may not have had all the knowledge or know-how they might have wished for. But faith in their ability to learn what they needed to know enabled them to remain confident in the face of challenge. Their confidence made them capable of leading themselves and their followers toward fulfillment of their vision for the future.

We all have our own story, our leadership path, and for most of us there are unforgettable people or significant events that helped shape us. You may be fortunate to have had someone in your life who encouraged or supported you, a person who would repeatedly let you know that you have what it takes to step up to leadership and succeed. Or, you may have developed an ardent belief in yourself and substantial confidence through diligent self-development, successfully facing challenges, or recovering from failures. The leaders in this book tell us there is no one, rigid path to success.

Belief in Yourself is Rooted in Your Uniqueness

Regardless of how your self-confidence developed, it is my personal belief that confidence ultimately results from a deep seated awareness of what makes you unique. That awareness may have been planted and nurtured in you by someone else. You may have attained it through the inner work of personal exploration and reflection, but the awareness is present; it's there. The self-confident leader knows that she is not a duplicate, nor will she be tempted to build or develop anyone in her image. Rather, she is truly one of a kind, put here to do what only she can do and in a way that only she can do it. Sara Blakely, the founder of Spanx and the youngest female billionaire at age 41, according to Forbes, epitomized that belief when she said, *"Don't be intimidated by what you don't know. That can be your greatest strength and ensure that you do things differently from everyone else."*

Belief in yourself involves understanding and accepting that you have the capacity and capability to do whatever it is that compels you from within. You may need more education, you may need to develop a new set of skills in a particular area, or you may need to find people who can give you wise counsel. But you already have everything within you to do what's required so you can advance toward your greatest dreams. Just like our twelve leaders who each found (and fostered) a firm belief deep within themselves, you, too, can find that belief if you haven't already done so. Like the bumblebee, you have no idea how far you can go until you fully apply your beliefs and abilities and move toward your dreams or goals with confidence.

For additional free personal development tools and information
on how you can create your unstoppable career visit
www.MyUnstoppableCareer.com

CORNERSTONE 2

COMMITMENT

The Three Fs of Commitment:

FIND
Your Jazz

FORGE
Ahead with Fortitude

FORTIFY
Your Foundation

CHAPTER 5

COMMITMENT: THE SECOND
LEADERSHIP CORNERSTONE

"Courage, sacrifice, determination, commitment, toughness, heart, talent, guts. That's what little girls are made of." —Bethany Hamilton

When you hear the word commitment, whose name comes to mind? For me, the twelve unstoppable women profiled in this book make the list. But before I'd met and interviewed them, there were some other women I thought of whose commitment to a personal calling have had an impact on us all—one being Candy Lightner.

Driven to Make a Change

You probably recognize her name. Candy's commitment to founding what would become one of the largest activist groups in the country, *Mothers Against Drunk Driving [MADD]*, causes my heart to beat a little bit faster. At the time she founded the organization in 1980, my own children were wee ones, but I could foresee the inevitable future when they'd be driving. Teen drivers and alcohol are a deadly mix, feeding every parent's fear that their child, even the most prudent, might one-day experiment and pay for it.

A car, when operated by a drunk driver, has an even greater potential to become a lethal weapon—not something I wanted my children to experience either as a victim or perpetrator. Therefore, when I first heard of the organization, I jumped on board to financially support its mission: tougher laws against offenders. As Lightner was quoted in *People* magazine, *"Death caused by drunk drivers is the only socially acceptable form of homicide."*

All of us have a calling, and how we experience that calling varies. Candy's calling and commitment was born from the tragic loss of her 13-year-old daughter Cari, who was savagely cut down by a *repeat* hit and run drunk driver while she was walking to a church carnival with a friend. Perhaps, like me, you find it heartbreaking to know Candy was informed by police that the offender would probably receive little or no jail time.[8]

Unfortunately, that wasn't the first time a drunk driver had significantly affected the Lightner family. At the age of three, Cari and her twin sister Serena were passengers in the family station wagon when it was rear-ended by a drunk driver, with Serena left bruised and cut. Then, six years later, Candy's four-year-old son Travis was playing outside in front of his home when he was run over by an unlicensed driver impaired by tranquilizers. Travis was left with multiple bodily injuries and permanent brain damage. Are you wondering what happened to the offending driver? He never even received a ticket.

Candy's rage over Cari's senseless death and a failure of the law to issue harsh penalties for drunk drivers and keep offenders off the road fueled her relentless commitment to creating tougher state and federal laws.

Candy Lighter travelled from her home state of California to Washington to raise awareness. She relentlessly hounded California Governor Jerry Brown's office until he launched a state commission on drunk driving with Candy appointed to the commission. She lectured extensively; she lobbied; she appeared on radio and major network television shows. She served on a number of other commissions and task forces; she rallied volunteers; she testified in Congress in favor of tougher drunk driving laws. This woman worked tirelessly to the exclusion of everything else. As she wrote in her book, *Giving Sorrow Words: How to Cope with Grief and Get on with Your Life*, *"I was unstoppable. I was so obsessed that, in many ways, I did not permit life to go on outside of MADD."* To say that Candy was committed may be an understatement—she was consumed by her cause.

The result of her obsession? In 1982 President Ronald Reagan invited her to serve on the National Commission on Drunk Driving. By 1984, the U.S. Congress had raised the national legal drinking age to 21, a move that saves an estimated 800 lives annually. Stiffer fines and penalties are now on the books across the country. Students Against Drunk Driving

[SADD], a spin-off organization founded by Lightner's daughter Serena, now has chapters across the continental United States.[9]

By 1999 MADD had become the largest victim-advocate and drunk driving activist organization in the world. According to the National Highway Traffic Safety Administration 2012 FARS data, in the United States, drunk driving deaths have been cut in half since the 1980 founding of MADD, saving over 300,000 lives and counting.

Candy Lightner's relentless commitment to heighten awareness, change laws, and get drunk drivers off the road took being willing to speak, lobby, and rally others to follow her lead. Her unstoppable efforts resulted in an international organization that has provided an immeasurable contribution to the welfare of people everywhere. Candy Lightner is considered a hero by many, certainly by me. One word defines her story and her mission: *Commitment.*

Commit to Commitment

Lou Holtz, retired Notre Dame football coach, ESPN sports analyst, and Football Hall of Famer, once said, *"If you don't make a total commitment to whatever you're doing, then you start looking to bail out the first time the boat starts leaking. It's tough enough getting that boat to shore with everybody rowing, let alone when a guy stands up and starts putting his life jacket on."* This is the kind of staying power that comprises the second leadership cornerstone: *Commitment.*

The Merriam-Webster online dictionary defines the word *commitment* as "a promise to be loyal to someone or something; the attitude of someone who works very hard to do or support something"[10] Note the two distinct components to this definition: the emotional component (loyalty) and the action component (hard work). This tells us that commitment is both a feeling and an undertaking; a feeling of fidelity and unflagging devotion to the promise you made. Commitment is a strong emotional bond which, when broken, prompts disappointment, regret, or, in some circumstances, despair. When you are totally committed to something (or someone), all your actions are focused on ensuring that your oath stands the test of time. Candy Lightner embodies both of these components, and so does an enduring leader.

The above definition of commitment certainly resonates with what

I learned about our twelve women leaders. Each embodied clarity and passion for a specific purpose. Each leader pursued her passion with courage and persistence, refusing to be stopped by difficult circumstances or obstacles in her way. In pursuit of her purpose, each leader focused on becoming the best she could be by overcoming or compensating for her weaknesses and enhancing her strengths. Each one of our leaders was willing to step out of her comfort zone and course correct where required, take risks, and make necessary sacrifices.

The Commitment Cornerstone

As you read about the commitment cornerstone, keep in mind that, while all twelve of our outstanding leaders were pursuing their purpose, each leader maintained internal alignment, resiliency, and faith in herself. It seems to me that character, that first cornerstone, enjoys a natural connection to commitment.

In contemplating the second cornerstone and its link to successful leadership, I found three distinct elements, depicted as:

The Three *Fs* of Commitment:

Find your jazz.
Forge ahead with fortitude.
Fortify your foundation.

THE DEPTH OF COMMITMENT

A single-minded focus, a relentless pursuit of excellence, and an unshakeable sense that nothing can stop you–this seems to be the mark of an unstoppable leader who achieves uncommon success. In the three chapters that follow, you will be introduced to three traits that fuel commitment. These qualities are what compel the most successful to hurl themselves out of bed every day, ready to face any challenge, brave any storm, and fight any dragon to achieve their goal, advance their mission, or fulfill their vision. Through the lives of our twelve unstoppable leaders, you will discover the power of finding your jazz—the compelling force that stirs your passion, fuels your fortitude, and galvanizes your endurance in the face of hurdles or hindrances.

CHAPTER 6

FIND YOUR JAZZ

"My philosophy is that not only are you responsible for your life, but doing the best at this moment puts you in the best place for the next moment." —Oprah Winfrey

Pat Summit, head coach emeritus for the Tennessee Women's Basketball Team, the Lady Vols, and holder of the most all-time wins for a men's or women's coach in NCAA basketball history, wrote: *"We keep score in life because it matters.... Too many people opt out and never discover their own abilities because they fear failure. They don't understand commitment. When you learn to keep fighting in the face of potential failure, it gives you a larger skill set to do what you want to do."*

Clearly, the world knew that Coach Summit was committed to excellence in every aspect of her sport, and she expected her players to be just as devoted. She believed in being committed to excellence with every fiber of her being. She expected a player to bring her entire self to every game, every single time. She believed in practice and discipline, and possessing a passion for being the best, consistently, hour after hour, day after day, week after week, game after game. Nothing less than total commitment was expected or tolerated. Coach Summit put it this way, *"If there is one thing I can't abide, it's lack of effort. I don't have much sympathy for people who act like they can't stand their jobs."* If there was one word that has encapsulated Pat Summit's life, like Candy Lightner, it has to be *commitment.*

You've probably heard this question: In a bacon and egg breakfast, what's the difference between the chicken and the pig? And the answer? *The chicken is involved, but the pig is fully committed!*

In any organization there's a place for involvement, but to lead at a level of uncommon success, commitment is an absolute requirement. Being committed to bringing the best of everything you have and applying it to every aspect of your job is a tall order, but when you consistently hold to your high standards, others notice. Consequently, people respect and trust deep, passionate commitment; it's something that can never be faked. The secret to finding the depth of commitment that prevails over the long haul hinges on *finding your jazz*, being involved in the work for which you hold the greatest passion. *Finding your jazz* is all about discovering your passion and pursuing it with your mind, body, and spirit, day in and day out.

Involvement or Commitment?

I once read this intriguing suggestion: *When faced with two choices, simply toss a coin. This works not because it settles the question for you, but because for that brief moment when the coin is in the air, you suddenly know what you are hoping for.* When your passion is in sight, you just know.

Our twelve featured leaders found their purpose and passion in life, and pursued it with excellence and endurance. Some of them spent years working in mind-numbing jobs or in areas where they didn't feel particularly skilled before they stumbled upon their real calling. But once their spirits were ignited, everything changed. They suddenly found themselves more charged, more motivated, and more fired up with energy. They threw themselves into their jobs, taking their newfound passion to heights they could hardly have imagined.

Mary Ellen Sheets spent two decades working in an uninspiring government job before she founded her business, Two Men and a Truck. She says, *"I was there twenty years, sitting in a cubicle day in and day out. I worked with some very nice people, but every day I looked at the clock in that cubicle and waited for my next vacation or my next coffee break. I couldn't wait to get off work. Then I became a business owner and I worked unbelievable hours. I worked until 3:00 in the morning. I would toss and turn all night and worry about employees, about everything. And I wouldn't trade that for anything. I loved it. It was mine."* What Mary Ellen described was commitment at its best.

Other women leaders have similar stories. Beth Jones always wanted to be a dentist, but found her true calling one day while reading the Bible. She received a revelation that her purpose was to take the message of God to people. It was a hard decision because she knew she would have to overcome male prejudices in the Church world in order to succeed. But her passion drove her to help establish and lead what would become one of the fastest growing mega churches in the country.

Kathie VanderPloeg studied to be a teacher, but quickly learned that she didn't like teaching, and wasn't particularly good at it either. She worked in her father's company through college to earn spending money and developed a keen interest in business, but completed her education degree and pursued teaching because that's what so many people were expecting her to do. It didn't take Kathie long to realize, however, that her real interest was in business.

Leaving the teaching profession was a difficult decision; she knew the financial sacrifices her parents had made to put her through college and that her choice would disappoint them. But the pull toward business was simply too great; she could not ignore the power of her passion. Kathie says, "*Sometimes the most difficult decision can also be the best decision we ever make because it helps us to get to the next place in our life—where we need to be. That's how I launched into the business. And now here I am—at the helm of the company.*" Commitment is an inner drive that feels impossible to ignore.

Similarly, Ruth Shaw spent decades in the academic community where she rose to senior administrator positions before leaping across the chasm into the unknown—the corporate world. She experienced her greatest success as a leader for Duke Energy, the country's largest utility, and became president and CEO of Duke Power Company, certainly a male-dominated industry. Her leadership ability and interests continually drove her to new levels of success.

Cheryle Touchton gave up her career in the music industry to become an entrepreneur in the field of IT. Discovering her gifts as a leader, she was propelled toward success by a passion for leading her company.

Each one of these women soared to new heights when she found her jazz and followed her passion, pursuing what she truly believed was her purpose in life. These women did not hesitate (at least not for long) to leave work they had outgrown so they could follow a deeper calling.

Pay Attention and Trust Your Instincts

I identify with the power of discovering passion and pursuing it. When my youngest child entered kindergarten, I knew that it was important for my family's well-being that I reenter the workforce. Because I began my career as a high school speech and English teacher, it seemed only natural that I'd return, despite a nagging, deep-seated sense that teaching was not what I wanted. Whenever I thought of returning to the classroom, I felt an unsettled feeling instead of inner peace.

Around the same time, my dear friend, Lyla Fox, gave my name to Sheila Hoffstetter, head of the medical library at a local hospital, who was looking for someone who could teach physicians and managers in the hospital how to design, develop, and deliver winning presentations.

After a brief interview, Sheila hired me on the spot. After finishing the series of classes, I was forever hooked on the profession of speaking and training and that's been my livelihood ever since. I had fallen into a position that opened the door to work that I love. One client engagement led to another, and continues to this day. I was blessed to create a career around public speaking, something I've been passionate about and committed to for over thirty years.

Purpose Fuels Passion and Vice Versa

Finding your jazz is a critical component to your success as a leader. It's not about a job. It's about finding your purpose and making a difference. What is it that drives you, motivates you, energizes you, and provides a passion that's hard to resist? If you've found it in your current work, you know it. If you jump out of bed in the morning feeling vitalized, invigorated, and excited to go to work, you've found your passion. On the other hand, if you get up every morning feeling reluctant, fatigued, or defeated before the day even begins, you have not *found your jazz*. Let me state clearly that this relates not only to work, but also personal pursuits you may have been pressured into thinking you "should" be doing.

Many years ago, I decided to take up yoga in order to feel fit and healthy. Yoga looked so simple; nice easy stretches, slow movements, a soft mat for performing the poses. It seemed the perfect exercise for me. Then I went to my first yoga class.

The yoga mat I had so blissfully bought failed to protect my bones from the hardwood floor beneath me. I was crushed. It felt as if I was the only person in the room who felt uncomfortable. What were these people made of? It felt as if I creaked and groaned with every pose and, frankly, that doggoned floor was assaulting my body. The core exercises burned my muscles so badly my limbs began to shake, and I could feel beads of perspiration dripping from my forehead while everyone else was calm and cool and in the zone.

This was an evening class and it had been a long day. Maybe I had come into the class too tired or too unprepared, but this was not my idea of fun. Even what I had fantasized as the "easy" poses turned torturous as I tried to stretch, twist, and relax all at the same time. Seriously? My mind played and replayed a very un-yoga like mantra, *"End this punishment! Flee now! Abandon this class! Lose this lousy, inadequate mat and disappear before someone talks you into signing up for a series!"*

But another recording was also playing in my mind. That one was my father's voice saying, *"Winners never quit and quitters never win."* Rats! I gutted it out and stayed until the bitter end, my energy lagging with every forced pose and stretch. Women near me, watching my obvious struggle, tried to be encouraging with, *"It gets easier with time."* I stayed because I needed to finish what I'd started, knowing full well that no one in that class would ever see me again.

The Empowerment of Passion

That yoga debacle reminded me that success at overcoming a challenge (physical or otherwise) ultimately begins and ends with how we perceive the challenge. It's no surprise that the activities I've stayed with, regardless of the pain or effort required to master them, have been pursuits for which I have a passion, such as what I do for my livelihood. I spent endless time, energy, and effort mastering the ability to capture and maintain the attention of an audience, and it didn't require spandex or a mat. I cultivated specific skills that help people transform in significant ways if they are willing to make desired changes to enhance their lives and work.

Through extensive study and practice, I honed my ability to tell stories that captivate people and get them involved in the action so they can see themselves performing more effectively. I learned how to help people discover the power within themselves so they can chart their own course, find their own voice, and discover their own solutions to obstacles that get in their way. And while yoga wasn't my thing, I support my physical self in other ways; daily walks rejuvenate and reenergize me, leaving me feel refreshed and invigorated.

I even learned to master social media as a means of getting my message of hope and inspiration out to thousands more than I might otherwise have had exposure. In other words, I am fully committed to doing whatever it takes to fulfill my calling of helping to ignite the greatness in others. My mission is to help leaders become unstoppable, better able to live their lives with joy, energy, and gratitude. I love what I do for a living and, because I am independently employed, I am free to pursue my career however I wish. My biggest reward is when people tell me working with me has been life-changing. I love finding out that my work with teams has resulted in deeper trust, making it possible for them to be more productive and work through conflict more effectively. It's a joy when an organization I've worked with experiences a massive turn around, resulting in happier employees, greater customer loyalty, and increased sales. The positive feedback, repeat and referral business (and a paycheck, of course) are nice, but that is not what drives me. It is the difference that my work is making for people, knowing that I am doing exactly what I am supposed to be doing.

Admittedly, yoga is not in my passion threshold—but helping people reach their potential by developing themselves and their leadership capacity is. Yoga depleted my energy and left me feeling like a failure (granted, I didn't give it much of a try). Inspirational speaking and transformational coaching, on the other hand, is where I find my jazz. Of course, there have been mistakes and failures along the way, but I never wanted to give up. As the leaders featured in this book have stated, finding your true calling fuels passion, and passion fuels commitment.

Open Up to Opportunity

But how do you discover your passion in the first place? Well, it all depends. One way to *find your jazz* is to explore your talents and be open to opportunities that come your way. Pay keen attention to what is going on in the world around you, and listen carefully to your customers and stakeholders. Find out if you have the skills or ability to fulfill a need in the marketplace or community. It can be said that our twelve women leaders certainly did that. Some of them stumbled upon their calling, some actively explored new, unfamiliar arenas, and some were so attuned to opportunity that when their purpose called out to them, they heard it and took action. But there are other avenues to *finding your jazz.*

When business owner Martha Mertz was invited to join the board at the Lansing Regional Chamber of Commerce, she wasn't too keen about it, as the board was made up entirely of males. Somewhat reluctantly she joined what appeared to be an "old boys" club and had difficulty relating to their views and work styles. But in this difficulty, she found opportunity, realizing that she could contribute to the board by bringing in a different perspective, her own, and later by bringing more women onto the board. Mind you, this wasn't easy. Initially, the men objected to her candidates because the women Martha presented were not really "leaders" by their definition.

They rejected the female candidates saying, *"Martha, she's not a leader."* Martha recognized that her colleagues' concept of leadership was that of the traditional male model. To them, a leader needed to be a business owner, corporate head, CEO, president, or chancellor. That certainly didn't jibe with Martha's concept. Although the women she introduced to the board were not heads of companies, they were leading people in their communities, schools and churches. They were making a difference in their chosen arenas and in different ways, inspiring others to take action in pursuit of powerful visions.

Martha saw a need in the community to recognize these women for their leadership and contribution. That was the genesis of the Chamber's ATHENA Award. Had Martha not witnessed the absence of women voices on her local Chamber board and made a commitment to address the issue, Martha might have remained just another name on a plaque listing former board members.

Instead, she is today the founder of a global movement. Since 1982, ATHENA International has awarded over 7000 women from over 500 communities and eight countries the ATHENA Leadership Award® for professional excellence, community service, and for providing exemplary leadership, assisting women in their professional development and

Be Willing to Stretch Yourself

Patricia Caruso never foresaw a career in criminal corrections. She was a county controller in Chippewa County, Michigan. As a county manager, she attended meetings that included representatives from the local prison in her county. The prison warden actively began recruiting Patricia when he recognized that her skills and competencies would be extremely useful to the Department of Corrections, and hired her as a business manager. Three years after joining the department, the director asked her to become a prison warden in Michigan's Upper Peninsula, a move widely viewed as controversial because Patricia had only been on the business side of operations, and in the department for just three years. She had never seen a prisoner's file in her life. Most people with such limited experience would have shied away from taking over the responsibility of a huge multi-level male prison. But not Patricia. She says, *"It worked out well. I ended up being the warden there for more than nine years. I loved it and would go back to being a warden."*

Patricia Caruso went on to become the first female director of the Michigan Department of Corrections and is widely known for her success in prison reform in Michigan. Under her leadership as the director, Michigan significantly reduced both its prison population and recidivism rate. Had Patricia not been open to the opportunity presented her to become a prison warden, she may never have found her true calling. *Finding your jazz*, your passion, requires that you are open to the possibilities around you, situations or needs that call out to you and stir you at a deep level.

Once you've *found your jazz*, heard the call of your real purpose, and identified your personal mission, does that mean it will be smooth sailing from there on? Of course not. Setbacks, failures, and mistakes are all part of everyone's life, including the uncommonly successful leader. The difference is that once you're in harmony with your jazz, you are much more likely to be able to face even the most difficult situations with energy and commitment. The professional lives of our twelve leaders make it clear that a passion for work is a key element of success. Regardless of setbacks, their passion keeps them committed to the task and makes their energy contagious, causing others to be moved and motivated by their example.

Passion Fuels Perseverance

Beth Jones's passion and devotion to her calling as a minister helped her persevere when beset with doubts generated by the unsolicited criticism she initially received as a female pastor. Her inner voice fueled her passion, speaking to her like a coach encouraging her to keep going and not quit. Martha Mertz, too, was driven by her passion to establish ATHENA International even when the going got tough. She says, *"It was a slow, arduous and sometimes painful process, but I certainly have learned how to pull from my passion in order to get my message across."*

If, despite exploring your talents and being open to opportunity, you haven't yet found your jazz, it may be because you need to be more attentive to what you say you want or to what your inner voice is telling you. Maybe you need more quiet time so you can clear away the clutter of busyness, anxiety, or fear so you can get in touch with your heart's desire. Sometimes the daily grind of making a living, and all that comes with it, can deafen us to that inner (or audible) voice that can turn us toward opportunity.

The Inner Voice of Purpose and Passion

Here's a prime example from a middle-aged labor attorney who plunked himself down in the seat next to me on a train heading home from Chicago. I thought that by keeping my nose buried in a novel he might get the clue, but clearly this man wasn't picking up on my signals. Acting as if he had my attention, Art (that was his name) commented, over my shoulder, on the blistering hot day and the surprisingly low number of passengers on the train. Having already noticed the empty seats, I wondered why he had chosen the spot next to me. Couldn't he see I wasn't interested in conversing with him?

To discourage further interaction, I barely grunted an acknowledgement and went back to my book. And then I heard him say, *"I think I'm having a mid-life crisis."* On that, I turned and looked squarely into his face. Now I was hooked. Whenever something gets personal, even from a stranger, it gets my attention.

He said he was depressed and, as a result, his work was getting progressively difficult to do. He had a chronic cough no doctor could explain. Whenever he'd begin to cough, he'd get depressed, put his paperwork away, lie down to rest, and then forget about his unfinished project. It was a routine he'd come to hate. I asked what seemed to be a reasonable question, *"Do you enjoy your work?"* After a long silence followed by several aborted attempts to answer the question, he mumbled, *"It's what I know."* Thinking that another approach might garner something more significant, I asked, *"If you could do anything you'd like to do, what would it be?"*

A single word, like a bullet, shot from his mouth, *"Writing!"* No need to think about that one. No hesitation. He knew.

"Fiction?"

"No, journalism."

"How much journalistic writing have you done in the past 10 years?"

"None. There's no time for it in my business."

The story was beginning to add up. His final statement was revealing. *"I hope you don't think I'm crazy,"* he said hesitantly, *"but I believe I have a powerful inner knowing, like ESP or something."*

"A powerful inner knowing, huh? How do you respond to it?"

"Well, I certainly don't encourage it. In my business, people are more interested in opinion based on facts. Sometimes it's pretty uncomfortable to have the facts pointing to one thing while inside you have this little voice telling you something else, especially when the little voice seems to always be right."

"Yes," I acknowledged, *"I can see where that could be uncomfortable."*

For almost three hours I listened to this stranger describe his inner struggles. I wanted to help him "fix it," but had the sense to know that wasn't my job, nor was it within my power. He needed to discover the answers for himself. All I could do was listen, ask questions that would get him to think more deeply about his plight and why it was happening. I hoped that maybe my questions would plant a few seeds.

When the conductor announced, *"Next stop, Kalamazoo,"* I knew I needed to act quickly.

"Did you ever think that maybe your body is trying to tell you something?" I asked. *"You say you are having a mid-life crisis. You say you love journalism, but haven't done any journalistic writing in the past 10*

years. You say you have an unexplainable cough that gets you depressed. You put things away and forget them, and then get more depressed. You say you have a powerful inner knowing that you tend to squelch. Sounds to me like your body is attempting to send you a strong message."

"You may have a point," he sighed.

As I stood up to leave, promising to send him some articles he might find useful, he reached out, touched my forearm, and said, *"Thanks, I really appreciated your taking time to listen to me."*

"You're welcome." I then added gently, *"But perhaps now it's time for you to begin to listen to yourself, to your inner voice. I have a strong suspicion that it's trying to tell you something, and you haven't been paying enough attention. You may want to pray for guidance, and listen closely. You just might get the answers you desire."*

Mitch Albom, best-selling author and radio and television broadcaster, once said, *"The way to get meaning into your life is to devote yourself to loving others, devote yourself to your community around you, and devote yourself to creating something that gives you purpose and meaning."* It didn't sound as if Art had been doing any of that; in fact, it seemed quite the contrary.

Clearly our twelve unstoppable leaders and others appearing in this book were committed to devoting themselves to something that has given them purpose and meaning. They followed their best instincts, listened to their inner (and sometimes audible voice) about what they wanted, or didn't want. They *found their jazz* and their commitment followed.

CHAPTER 7

FORGE AHEAD WITH FORTITUDE

*"There is no chance, no destiny, no fate
that can hinder or control the firm resolve of a
determined soul." —Ella Wheeler Wilcox*

Arriving home from a speaking engagement in Columbus, Ohio just in time to watch the opening kickoff in a game between the Chicago Bears and the Green Bay Packers, I didn't miss a play. Though one of my favorite pro teams lost (Bears 27, Packers 20), I was again reminded of the commitment demonstrated by the man considered to be one of the greatest football coaches of all time—Vince Lombardi. In his book, *What It Takes to be Number One,*[11] Coach Lombardi wrote: *Winning is not a sometime thing; it's an all the time thing. You don't win once in a while; you don't do things right once in a while; you do them right all of the time. Winning is a habit. Unfortunately, so is losing.*

Lombardi was committed to excellence in every aspect of his sport, and, like Pat Summit, he expected his players to be just as devoted. Lombardi believed that brains were important to being number one in any type of business, but there was one thing he prized as greater than brain. He valued heart; being totally committed to excellence. This was the secret of Vince Lombardi's success as a coach and the success of the champions he created and nurtured. Lombardi exemplified, and instilled in his players, the quality of fortitude, especially under pressure.

Aristotle included fortitude in the four Cardinal Virtues—Prudence, Justice, Fortitude and Temperance. Fortitude, commonly called *courage*, is an inner strength of mind and spirit that enables a person to face danger, overcome fear, and endure pain or adversity to do what needs to be done. While finding your jazz is essential to leadership success, and being resolute in pursuit of your passion is a requirement to greatness, it is fortitude that keeps you going. Fortitude allows you to experience setbacks and mishaps without being deterred from your mission. *Forging ahead with fortitude* requires more than buoyancy, resilience, and flexibility. It requires a level of endurance that takes you out of your comfort zone to the point that you take risks and make bold decisions. It requires that you stay on purpose with a single-minded focus and, in some situations, summon new levels of courage. Our women leaders are prime examples of pursuing their enduring passions with courage and fortitude.

Run Your Own Race

As a long-time fan of Marlo Thomas, I rushed to buy her book, *The Right Words at the Right Time,* the very month it hit the bookshelves[12]. Her introductory story grabbed me and never let go. It described how she went to her famous father, Danny Thomas, to tell him she wanted to change her last name so she would not constantly be compared to him. He told her, *"I raised you to be a thoroughbred. When thoroughbreds run they wear blinders to keep their eyes focused straight ahead with no distractions, no other horses. They hear the crowd, but they don't see it.… They just look ahead and run their own race."*

The next night, at the theater where she was performing, the stage manager delivered a package to Marlo's dressing room. Inside was a pair of old horse blinders with a note that read, *"Run your own race, Baby."*

That story has spoken volumes to me personally. Many times over the past twenty years I have had moments when I was tempted to give up my "Big Dream" of being a nationally accredited keynote speaker at conferences and conventions across the country, able to share my message of hope and inspiration with multitudes. After all, the combination of skills, abilities, and hard work required to develop the reputation and maintain momentum can be overwhelming. It would have been much easier to remain content being a breakout speaker and trainer. But I was drawn by my passion and desire; I was driven to pursue that dream, and simply could not give up. I had to persevere. It's hard to express my exhilaration over bringing my dream to fruition—and how blessed I feel as a result. Your big rewards come from *forging ahead with fortitude* on the road to realizing your dream when it would be far easier to give up or get complacent.

Fortitude: A Powerful Fuel

Achieving purpose is a lifelong journey, and it requires us to be in it for the long haul. It calls for marathon runners, not sprinters. If we remain a sprinter we might quit when the going gets tough and the journey seems longer and takes more time and hard work than we ever bargained for or expected. Marathon runners know that there will be pain along the way, there will be times when they feel like quitting, but by staying the course, the time will come when they get into the "zone" and their legs take over, knowing what to do. With the finish line in sight, those legs press on, knowing that the reward will be worth the pain of the journey. That is fortitude. Challenge, challenge, challenge—win!

La June Tabron says, *"What got me to where I am today is my perseverance. The fact that I was able to work in such a complicated organization over a period of twenty-seven years, and seemed to work all that time with a pretty stellar reputation, building friendships, and establishing a level of credibility and integrity in order to get to the top leadership role took perseverance."* She later added, *"So [what is important is] knowing deeply what works for you, and staying true to your North Star and not allowing circumstances to drive you off course..."*

Kathie VanderPloeg's success journey at Ship-Pac was also *forged with fortitude.* When she encountered negative family dynamics in the business owned by her father and run by Kathie and her two brothers, she could have given up hope of ever leading the company. A lesser leader might have bailed, but Kathie persevered. She knew what was good for the business and for its people, and she was determined to see her passion, purpose, and plan through.

Even though she believed that her father secretly expected her younger brother to take over the business when the three siblings would be given their chance to prove their mettle, it didn't work that way. Kathie devised a sustainable business plan, put together a winning financial model, developed a support system, and received buy-in from the stakeholders. Kathie then boldly presented her plan and strategy to the board that would choose the person best suited to run the business when their father retired. This called for a great deal of persistence and hard work. Passion's faithful companion is fortitude because without fortitude, your passion may end up as a hobby rather than a lifelong pursuit as it has been for Kathie and the other women leaders who have achieved uncommon success.

Beth Jones faced heaps of resistance as a female pastor in an evangelical church. At one point, she was forced to throw what she calls "gutter balls" and downplay her skills and talents, something she learned to do as a kid. She talks about bowling with boys and girls from her neighborhood when she was in the seventh grade. Her mom would warn Beth and her friends, *"Girls, make sure you don't beat the boys when you go bowling."* Though she bowled well, Beth forced herself to throw gutter balls whenever she felt she was at risk of beating the boys. Throwing gutter balls didn't end with seventh grade; it followed her into her adult life and her church work. For years she continued this adaptive behavior, downplaying her talents to avoid appearing better than her male colleagues. She now realizes this was a waste of time, and she tells the girls she mentors, *"Don't do what I did, which was being a reluctant leader and throwing gutter balls so I didn't overachieve. That wasn't a good choice. If God has given you gifts and has called you to be a leader, be wise and go for it!*

Fortitude takes soldiering on, putting one foot ahead of the other, showing up at work, facing whatever forces come against you—naysayers, criticism, fear, or negativity. It requires the grit to keep going, even when every fiber of your being is crying to give up! It requires a singular focus on your goal. It requires you to ignore negative people and the little voice inside your head that keeps saying, *"This is insane—you cannot do this."* The leader is required to act courageously every day, to overcome her personal fears so she can focus on her purpose.

Mary Ellen Sheets, for example, talks about the early days of her business when she battled nervousness and shyness. Her anxiety at times was so extreme that people called her "Pinky" because she blushed so much. It was difficult for her to talk to people, especially if it required her to speak up in public. She would look at her feet and blush. She lacked in self-confidence, in part because she was a divorced woman, and, in part because people in her workplace made fun of her "little business." Mary Ellen knew, however, that if she wanted to have a successful business, she'd need social skills for meeting people and interacting in groups. She would need to force herself out of her comfort zone.

Her passion—her belief in what she felt she was put on this earth to pursue—took precedence, so she did everything she needed to do in spite of the difficulty. She says, *"The first thing I did as a new business owner was to join the Chamber of Commerce. I started meeting people. I made myself get out there and pass out those business cards."* Mary Ellen simply refused to allow inhibition to stand in her way. Through acts of courage—fortitude—she was successful in overcoming her lack of confidence and bashfulness. She simply tried to remember that everyone gets nervous at times, and if she would do something enough, it would get easier. Mary Ellen had made a commitment to herself and to the success of her business, and she wasn't going to let anything stop her.

Martha Mertz had to conquer her fear of public speaking in order to pursue her purpose. There was a time when Martha was terrified of having to face a group of people and speak about her desire for having more gender balance in leadership. However, she, too, now speaks with confidence and poise in front of hundreds of people. Martha had to conquer her fear again and again in order to convey her message, but she did it. She says, *"If I hadn't been willing to face that fear every single time until it finally melted away, ATHENA International probably wouldn't exist today. I had to grow enough to be able to make this happen."*

On the other hand, the challenge might be in stepping forward when the opportunity arises and having the courage to handle what follows. This is what Mary Ellen Rodgers did when she moved to West Michigan as a young partner with Deloitte and was looking for more responsibility—she was ready to move on to the next stage of her career. She knew she needed to step out and proactively seek opportunity rather than waiting for it. She said, *"It sort of takes all that you have within you to tell your boss, 'You know what, I think I am ready to do something else... to do more.' I was very young; I think I was 36 at the time. I had two young children, ages seven and three, and I knew that if I raised my hand and said, 'I am ready to do something else; I want to be a leader here,' there was a great likelihood I was going to have to move. This is exactly what happened within about an eight-week period."*

Mary Ellen knew, at the same time, that uprooting her husband and kids would take time, energy, and effort, and yet it was a transition she was willing to undertake because she was committed to what she believed was her purpose and her passion. She says, *"It was tough, but I think if you are true to what you want to do, and if you are clear about what is palatable for you from a personal perspective, and where the line is that you can't go over, then it becomes easier. You have to have your own personal North Star."* None of us can know the sacrifices Mary Ellen made, nor the time and energy she put into making her decision, but the fact is she was committed to her personal North Star, and she *forged ahead with fortitude* to follow it.

Some of us get blocked when facing fear, sometimes for years, due to lack of fortitude. Only when we have the courage to "feel the fear and do it anyway" can we forge our way toward uncommon success. Giving in to immobilizing fear, on the other hand, can only lead to regret. As a very young woman, I still remember a time I allowed fear to stop me, and it is something I regretted for a long time.

Fear Foils Opportunity

I was on my way to the Federal Center in Detroit so I could take the test for my third-class radio license, a requirement for becoming a radio announcer at a small station in Whitehall, Michigan where I'd been promised a job spinning records for the summer. It was a beautiful day in May, the month of my twentieth birthday, and I was excited about the possibilities that lay ahead for me in the world of broadcasting. Over 200 people sat for the test that day, and I was the only female in the room.

That same year, I served as an ambassador for the National Cherry Industry, and on the heels of learning I'd passed the licensing test, I went on a weeklong tour across the United States and Canada, representing Michigan's Cherry Growers. We traveled from Montreal to Vancouver and then to Los Angeles, where a group of us were invited to attend the Lawrence Welk Show and to be guests the following night at the Hollywood Palladium where Mr. Welk's band was playing.

That night Welk's long-time announcer, Ralph Portner, graciously asked me to dance. In answer to his questions, I explained that I was a college student about to begin my summer job as an announcer on a local radio station back home. He told me that I'd need a radio name and suggested I use *MJ, Your Private DJ*. I liked the sound of it and told him so. He then added, *"You'll also need something to set you apart. I'm going to send you Words of Wisdom, a book of quotations. Every day, end with a good one.*

You can sign off each show by saying, 'This is MJ, Your Private DJ, signing off with a word of wisdom.' Then share the quotation." I was amazed and flattered by the personal interest he took in me.

Following that trip, wherever Lawrence Welk's Band was working, whether in Lake Tahoe or Reno or LA, Mr. Portner would send me a quick postcard. *"Hi Stranger — Face getting brighter – pockets lighter — truly beautiful country,"* or *"How's your progress? Have been gorging on the big Bing cherries – and I love 'em – Show going over 'real big' – Best of thoughts–Sincerely, Ralph Portner"* or, on several occasions, an encouraging letter. Much to my regret, I never wrote back.

Because of my own insecurity, I was afraid that if I wrote to him, he'd discover that I wasn't the person he thought I was and would change his mind about any talent he might have seen in me. And so I allowed my fear to stand in the way of stepping into what I thought was the opportunity that he was offering me at a very young age to be mentored by one of the best voices on radio and TV. Eventually, Mr. Portner stopped writing.

Decades have passed since then and not a year has gone by that I don't think of the gift he'd held out to me, and how I, out of fear, neglected to accept his gift, learn what I could, and grow from it. The good news is that my deepest regret turned into the impetus that drove me to make cold calls when starting my own business over twenty-five years ago. It took every ounce of courage in me to pick up that phone and call. But, I was committed to the task. Experience had taught me to forge ahead in the face of fear and do it anyway—or I would come to one-day regret it.

Leaders Face Their Fears

Leaders are not blocked or stopped by fear. It's not that they never experience it; indeed, they do. Instead of giving in to fear, effective leaders choose to face their fear and take action in spite of it. When a door of opportunity opens, they step through that door, realizing they have all that's needed inside themselves to take advantage of what is being made available to them. When performance insufficiencies demand new approaches to situations and changes have to be made, leaders are able to identify and confront their fears so they don't immobilize themselves or render their organizations vulnerable. Sometimes leaders have to make hard choices that require them to give up one thing in order to try another way of operating, but they realize that they cannot move forward while looking backward; that it's mandatory to give up the known to move toward a more promising future.

My dad was famous for saying to us while growing up, *"Plan your work and work your plan—and don't let anything stand between you and what you believe you are here to do."* I'm not sure what our twelve women leaders heard from their homes growing up, but somehow they grasped the importance of *forging ahead with fortitude.*

CHAPTER 8

FORTIFY YOUR FOUNDATION

*"Learn everything you can, anytime you can, from
anyone you can – there will always come a time
you will be grateful you did." —Sarah Caldwell*

T he subject of this book is women leaders, but I'd be remiss if I didn't
mention a male leader I met over twenty-five years ago who was
also committed to excellence—John Brown, the retired president,
CEO, and now Chairman Emeritus of Stryker Corporation. I'd just started
my business and didn't know enough to be fearful of contacting a CEO
directly. I simply called his number before opening hours when he was
more apt to answer his own phone, which he did. Mr. Brown agreed to
a meeting.

Our conversation during the meeting was brief. He asked how he could
help me, and I ignorantly responded with, *"Mr. Brown, do you believe
in training your people?"* He looked at me inquisitively, leaned forward
and asked me a question of his own, *"What do you know about our company?"* All I knew was that Stryker was the company that manufactured
the famous Stryker hospital bed. I fumbled at a response. He leaned over
and pressed a button, calling for his administrative assistant, *"Judy, please
bring me the latest financial figures."*

His assistant appeared in the doorway and handed Mr. Brown some
papers. He looked through them, pulled one out, and held out a chart that
illustrated the growth of the company. *"See this,"* he said, pointing to a bar
on a bar chart. *"This is where we were when I took over the company."* And
then he added, *"And here is where we are today. We've had better than a
20% growth rate every single year since I took over this position. And you
ask me if I believe in training?"* My heart began to pound and my mind

172

raced for something to say. I was totally unprepared for this meeting. All I managed was, *"Wow! It sounds like you expect 100% from your people."* To which the CEO responded, *"No, I expect 110%—every day."*

I left Mr. Brown's office with a valuable lesson that day: If I wanted to rise to the top in my own field, I needed to exhibit commitment to excellence. The standard couldn't be just now and then, but every single day. In case you don't know, John Brown's name was synonymous with 20% growth in sales for the three-plus decades he sat at Stryker's helm. Like Pat Summit and Lou Holtz, John Brown engendered trust in stockholders and employees alike with an unrelenting commitment to being the best. Even Stryker's tag line emphasized this commitment—*First be best, then be first.*

First Be Best

Being the best does not necessarily refer to being better than others. Rather, it means giving your personal best to whatever it is you want to achieve. Forging ahead with fortitude only works when you have *fortified your foundation* with the competence, mindset, and skills that will take you to the top. Besides continuously improving and refining the skills you have already honed, it's important that you identify the competencies that need strengthening. From there, you consistently work on them while bringing people onto your team with skills in areas that will fill the gaps. When interviewing the Unstoppables, something stood out for me—they have all been intentional at developing competencies that allowed them to excel.

Their commitment to lifelong excellence was clearly a trait that helped propel them to the top of their field. Even in my own business, it's always the best-of-the-best who show up at every conference or educational meeting and sit in the front row with pen and paper, or computer, and take notes, sharpening their skills and building on their competencies. Those who aspire to reach the top of their field never stop learning, and they delight in teaching others by their examples.

Lillian Bauder epitomizes the intentional achiever, the quintessential learner. She constantly demands her best, and for good reason. According to Bauder, when you work hard to be the best at what you are currently doing, it opens doors to the future, to the next level of responsibility. And Lillian is living proof of that belief. Though, as a young woman, she never aspired to be what she eventually became, her quest for excellence in everything she did led to other opportunities. Each time she moved up, Lillian enhanced her capacity to take on larger leadership roles and solve bigger and more complex problems. It didn't take long for her to learn that she loved this ongoing growth process.

She says, *"I'd like to tell women not to aspire to be a great leader, but instead, do the best that you can every day, in every role that you play. I mean that in terms of being a good friend, a good everything—be the best that you can be."* Being committed to bringing your best to everything you do isn't an easy habit to cultivate. But, when you consistently operate at this level, others notice, and with that notice, they generally bring their respect and trust. That level of performance is something that cannot be bought, faked, or forced. It speaks volumes about you, and for you.

The Best Leaders are the Best Learners

Being your best consistently requires a mind-set of seeking continuous learning and growth. Each one of the women I interviewed emphasized the importance of ongoing learning and its role in their success as a leader. Almost all of them invest time in reading—books, articles, and newspapers—to ensure that they remain current in their own field and with what's happening in the world. Some of them have gone the extra mile by obtaining advanced degrees and certificates of learning in areas where they felt they needed to know more. Others created and participated in group discussions with other like-minded people in their own and other fields.

Lillian Bauder, in particular, talks about her love of learning not just from books, but from people from all walks of life. She says, *"I like to keep learning; it is just part of who I am. I have learned tremendously from all sorts of individuals at all levels of life; I value them and respect them. I believe this is a crucial quality of effective leaders as well."*

Our women leaders spent a lot of time learning new skills and finessing them so they could overcome their weaker or undeveloped areas. Many forced themselves to learn critical skills that helped them facilitate a quantum leap in their careers. For instance, when Cheryle Touchton was asked to step into the role of CEO of a cutting-edge software start-up company, she realized that, *"first and foremost you have to be competent at what you are doing."* Working with highly intelligent Ph.D. engineers, it was imperative to her that she excel in every area of leadership, and she began taking classes to receive her MBA. She freely admits to this day, *"I am constantly taking classes because I believe I need to always be improving myself."* Consider how Martha Mertz, terrified of meeting new people and making public speeches, overcame that weakness by forcing herself to go out and meet people.

Similarly, Ruth Shaw focused on overcoming her hesitation in stepping into new situations by reminding herself that she was capable of learning, while Mary Ellen Sheets forced out her shyness and nervousness in meeting people by putting herself in positions where she had to interact socially, again and again. Gail McGovern struggled with her inability to fire people until it was something she could do comfortably and competently. In each situation, these women found a way to fortify their foundation so they could capably do the very things that could have prevented them from becoming successful leaders.

Other Sources of Learning: Models and Mentors

On the other hand, Martha Mertz talks about learning from what she calls "reverse role-models." According to her, sometimes her best lessons come from negative examples; people who exhibit behaviors and work styles she doesn't want to emulate. Martha says, *"Learning from relationships around us—whether negative or positive—is something that truly great leaders must consistently and continuously do."* What she says is true. Good and bad models of management and leadership abound in every workplace as well as in the media. We can learn from them all.

Another important method of learning is through mentors. Each of our twelve women leaders had mentors of one kind or another they could learn from, whether a supervisor, colleague, friend, or family member. Kathie VanderPloeg had an independent board of directors that guided and advised her through every major business decision and difficulty she faced. Gail McGovern seeks out mentors from different walks of life to support her in her journey. Mary Ellen Sheets described her franchise attorney as one of her first mentors, and perhaps the most important one. He helped her take her business from a local one-woman show to the level of an international franchise.

Mary Ellen Rodgers speaks at length about the importance of having a "personal board of directors." She suggests having a set of mentors who can support you in various areas, made up of people from different parts of the organization, people with different strengths and different skills that you can trust and seek advice from when facing major challenges. According to Rodgers, the personal board of directors must also include a few individuals who have no connections with the business, people with whom you can vent, and those who will listen without judging or offering advice. These are most likely the ones who can make you laugh and take your mind off your work stress when you most need the relief.

Mentoring at its most basic is advising, passing on knowledge, skills, or wisdom learned from experience, but at its best, it is much more. And based on those who have made it to the top, it's something you do not want to be without.

Being Your Best Takes Work

Most people will never see the hard work and effort a powerful leader puts into overcoming a weakness or building on strengths to fortify their foundation. The only thing others may see is the result of all that hard work, making it all look so natural and effortless to the casual observer. But there is a wealth of time, energy, and effort that goes into reaching that level of skill. My son brought this message home to me by something he said after hearing me deliver a keynote address a few years ago.

A local philanthropic organization that supports women's higher education invited me to keynote their major fundraiser. They titled the event "Hogs and Kisses," derived from my book, *You CAN Teach a Pig to Sing– Create Great Relationships...with Anyone, Anytime, Anywhere.*

If you've done any public speaking, you know that audiences can run warm or cool, and a group's readiness to receive your message is half the battle. A "hot" audience (one that is ready and receptive) is a speaker's dream. Well, all of the stars must have been aligned, because this Saturday morning's audience was *blazing hot.* Not only does a good speaker energize an audience, a good audience energizes the speaker, and we were a perfect fit from the moment I began, making it easy for me to be at my finest.

After the accolades had been shared and the crowd had left, my husband, my son, his girlfriend, and I headed back to our house. Sitting on our screened-in porch, enjoying Michigan's rare late November sunshine, we chatted about a variety of things. Then, out of the blue, my son said, *"Mom, I thought your program this morning was fabulous! I was so proud that you were my mother. You made it all look so easy. But I know something all those other people who attended don't know. I know the years of time and energy you've put into becoming so good at what you do. I know the sacrifices you've made to become one of the best speakers I've ever heard. And I'm not just saying that because you're my mom. You're a masterful speaker. I know how hard you've worked, and I've learned from you that if I want to get good at anything, I'm going to have to work at it. It isn't just going to happen overnight. I may have to work years to get that good. And, Mom, that's just about the best lesson I think I could ever learn. Getting excellent and being successful doesn't come without effort—and lots of it. I've learned that, and I have you to thank for it."*

It was exhilarating to hear such high praise from my son. I never realized he was watching so closely. But he was. He was observing, taking in, and learning, not from anything I said, but from what I did. He was there, witnessing and remembering all those days, weeks, and years of work I had put into mastering my craft.

My father, who was raised on a dairy farm, used to say, *"Never worry about how many people there are who do what you do. Just remember, the cream always rises to the top. You just have to make sure that you're part of the cream."* Our twelve women leaders certainly are part of the cream that rises to the top, and each of them know the time and sacrifice and energy that was required to get there.

Fortify from the Foundation Up

When I think about the genesis of leadership and growing the skills it takes to be the best, I can't help but think of the bamboo tree. The seedling is planted, and for five years it needs to be watered and fertilized regularly. Nothing appears to be happening while the seed lies there, buried in the soil all that time. However, once the seedling finally matures and emerges above the ground in the form of a sprout, the plant can grow to a height of 90 feet in just six weeks. Can you imagine, ninety feet in just six weeks! How does this happen? Well, during that five years the seed spends underground, it is busy building its foundation, an elaborate root system that enables the tree to grow like crazy in just six weeks.

Those who lose sight of their dream and forsake their passion never realize that they must nurture and cultivate their desire by building a foundation; taking classes to grow in knowledge and skill, constantly flooding themselves with positive thoughts and insights, finding ways to support other people's efforts, getting mentors, building alliances, whatever it takes.

This concentrated effort puts emerging and developing leaders on a continuous growth path, moving them closer to their true calling, to their heart's deepest desire, and the development of their true potential. Leaders who achieve uncommon success do this over and over again throughout their careers.

An organization is only as good as its leaders because it's the leaders who set the bar for the level of excellence expected in the organization. People are always watching, always aware, and always following the leader's example. *Fortifying your foundation* is all about excellence; it's about setting the bar high, and continuing to reset the bar as you grow and develop, with no real end in sight. Our women leaders know without a doubt that they are the ones who set the bar for any who may follow.

If you have any questions about how you can supercharge your career, feel free to contact me at **MaryJane@MaryJaneMapes.com**

CORNERSTONE

CORE WORK

The Three Cs of Core Work:

CREATE
and Execute a Compelling Vision

CRAFT
a 3-C Team

CULTIVATE
Critical Relationships

CHAPTER 9

CORE WORK: THE THIRD LEADERSHIP CORNERSTONE

*"There are no short cuts to any place
worth going." –Beverly Sills*

A friend of mine told me about a fascinating comeback story that stuck with me. After both being inspired and wondering if her report was accurate, I was able to find out more with a quick Internet search for Frank O'Dea.

Frank O'Dea, Founder of Second Cup, one of Canada's largest coffee house franchises, is someone people from outside Canada may not have heard of, but thousands of Canadians have been inspired by his life. As a child, Frank was sexually abused and, in time, he turned to alcohol to numb his traumatic past. Frank's family relationships deteriorated to the point that his father had to lay down the law. *"Straighten up or get out,"* he told his son.

Frank left home and became a panhandler, sleeping on park benches and working menial jobs to earn enough money for a drink. One day, listening to the radio, he heard about a rehabilitation program. This was the pivotal moment for Frank, who vowed to turn his life around, and he did. In time, he founded Second Cup and a series of other businesses and international not-for-profit organizations. Today he shares his story with thousands of people annually, giving a message of hope to others who are down and out or struggling through life.

In his book, *When All You Have is Hope*[13] Frank repeatedly talks about two essential elements that helped him move from failure to fortune. One of these elements was *vision* and the other was *hope*. For Frank, vision, and the hope his vision inspired, marked the beginning. To change the trajectory of his life from that of a homeless drifter to international business owner, philanthropist, and globe-trotting speaker, required a willingness to do the core work needed to move toward his vision.

Frank's story brings us to *Core Work*, the third cornerstone of a great leader. Central to the core work of any exceptional leader is vision, which leads the way to the work that needs to be done, and hope, which is the positive expectations of things to come. These two elements fuel core energy, not just for the inspired leader, but for those who adopt the leader's vision.

Although each of our unstoppable leaders acted in a manner that was consistent with her personal values and style, like Frank, each had to discover who she was and what she was all about. With a deep understanding of herself, each leader did the work necessary for the accomplishment of her vision. My interviews with the twelve women presented in this book offer a good deal of insight into what constitutes core work. Reading through each leader's profile, you have no doubt come to the conclusion that these twelve women and their personal journeys are different in many ways. Yet they all share some common personal traits and professional practices when it comes to the core of their work. I describe the three essential elements of the third leadership cornerstone, *Core Work*, in the form of The Three Cs.

The Three *Cs* of Core Work:

Create and execute a compelling vision.
Craft a 3-C team.
Cultivate critical relationships.

THE HEART OF A LEADER'S CORE WORK

The chapters in this section describe the core work of a leader, but do not provide an exhaustive list of core functions. Rather, they reflect three significant components of what it takes to lead with both effectiveness and efficiency, creating an environment where trust is high and teamwork thrives. Central to a leader's core work is a compelling vision—the purpose or future envisioned for transforming the organization, inspiring employees to take action and live the vision at every opportunity. Every manager might claim to want a well-working team with members who are competent, skilled and knowledgeable, but it takes strategy to make that happen. In crafting a team, it's critical to get the right mix of individuals where you can cultivate the kind of spirit that sustains the team. Finally, you'll see why and how fostering relationships truly is the bedrock of successful leadership.

CHAPTER 10

CREATE AND EXECUTE A COMPELLING VISION

"A vision is not just a picture of what could be; it is an appeal to our better selves, a call to become something more." –Rosabeth Moss Kanter

As children we learn that caterpillars turn into butterflies, but not everyone knows about the life cycle of moths. Enter the Processionary Caterpillar. The French entomologist Jean-Henri Fabre` was fascinated by this furry insect because of its instinct to blindly follow whatever caterpillar is in front of it. Traveling in a single line, the caterpillars attach themselves front to back, forming a single column in search of food. Wherever the first caterpillar goes, all others follow.

Fabre` conducted an experiment placing several caterpillars in a single continuous loop around the circumference of a flowerpot. He then set a food source just inches away, wanting to see how long it would take the caterpillars to break away from the line and head for the food. To his astonishment, it didn't happen. Even with food so close, the caterpillars continued circling, following the same pattern for a *week*, until they began dying from exhaustion and starvation.

Fortunately, we human beings are more intelligent and have better instincts than caterpillars. Most of us, at some point, are unwilling to follow a leader who either expects blind loyalty or one who doesn't know where she (or he) is going. To do our best work, we need and want a leader who has a clear vision, who communicates it effectively, and inspires us to embrace and work toward fulfilling the vision. Otherwise, we make the choice to pursue a different direction.

The *Book of Proverbs* states that where there is no vision, the people perish. If you study ancient civilizations that fell, leaving only ruins behind, you know these words are true. The same can be said of organizations: Where there is no vision, organizations perish. Vision is what inspires the reality. Truth be told, everything that has been created, whether organizations, breakthrough inventions, or social movements, everything first began as a vision in somebody's mind.

The Power of Vision

Consider Walt Disney who had a vision of his Magic Kingdom. Some say he saw it in a dream, while others say he imagined it and put everything down on paper, right down to the design of Sleeping Beauty's Castle. Martin Luther King articulated his vision in his speech when he said, *"I have a dream that one day my four children will live in a country where they will be judged not by the color of their skin, but by the content of their character."* His dream changed the course of history in the United States.

Mahatma Gandhi had a vision for India as a nation free from British rule. Steve Jobs had a vision of a personal computer on everyone's desk, visualizing innovative, quality products focused on unique design and quality customer experiences. Mary Kay Ash's dream was one of women being given the opportunity to go as far as their ability could take them— to become the best they could be. Mary Kay believed that women were unique and special and could succeed beyond their wildest dreams.

Billionaire Sara Blakely, creator of Spanx, a hosiery company that specializes in undergarments and bodysuit shapewear, attributes her success to creating a vision and writing it down on paper. Larry Page and Sergey Brin, big vision thinkers who co-founded the world's most popular search engine, Google, in 1998, have yet to achieve their ultimate vision: to organize the world's information and make it universally accessible and useful. Larry shared this vision and what's yet to be done in a 2014 TED Talk.[14]

This is but a sample of leaders with big visions who communicated their ideas so clearly and so passionately that they inspired leagues of others to follow them or to participate in what they created. Just imagine the number of lives who were permanently changed or positively influenced by this handful of visionary thinkers.

Vision Sets the Course

People in positions of authority only become true leaders when they have a vision of the direction in which they want to take their unit, team, or organization. Vision requires the ability to see something that initially exists only in the domain of the imagination. From there, the effective leader communicates and behaves consistently and persistently in a manner that engages others and drives the team toward making the vision a reality. Of course, "vision" means having a clear picture of the end in mind, regardless of what you intend to create.

On stages and platforms across the country, I often speak on the importance of having a vision for improving the relationships in your life. In an interview with Shelley Irwin of WGVU radio in Grand Rapids, Michigan on the subject of my 2011 book, *You CAN Teach a Pig to Sing – Create Great Relationships with Anyone, Anytime, Anywhere,* she asked me, *"What is one thing people can do if they want to transform difficult relationships?"* That was easy. Visualize the relationship you want, and then begin acting and behaving as if you already have it. Of course, the power to visualize and then act to bring about the outcomes you desire is not restricted to transforming relationships. The process and practice is exactly the same for *anything* you want to achieve, from parenthood to sports performance to health improvement. Create the vision; keep it in front of you, and practice taking the steps that will make your vision a reality.

Our brains have a tremendous capacity for visualization. In fact, your eyes take in approximately four million bytes of information per second, processing, and forming pictures in your mind's eye. For example, if I were to write the words, "flying eagle," you wouldn't simply see the words. Your mind would instantly conjure a picture of a soaring eagle based on your memory bank of images or experiences, whether from a book, an actual sighting, or a TV nature documentary. You have the ability to picture almost anything in your mind's eye.

Try this right now. Stop reading for a moment and visualize someone you love or something that makes you smile. Now imagine something you want to achieve, change, or make happen. That same aptitude, your ability to visualize from the past, present, and even into the future, plays a key role in what you are able to achieve. From conception comes birth. The mental pictures you carry around in your mind every day have an uncanny way of materializing. This is why some people caution: *"Be careful what you think about."* It is my hope that you have a vision of who and what you want to be with glimmers of how to get there. Hang onto those thoughts; systematically shape and nurture them. You have no idea what your potential is until you give it a try. The same goes for the vision you have for your team or organization.

Vision Fuels the Future

It's a privilege and pleasure to be personally acquainted with a few of the women I interviewed for this book. Beth Jones, one of the two senior pastors of the church I attend, is one such woman. Twenty-five years ago Beth and her husband had a vision of growing a large church where members of the congregation would deeply understand the fundamentals of their faith. Even when there weren't enough people to fill the seats, you could drive by the church and see some friendly faces directing traffic in the parking lot. Beth and her husband were "acting as if" they had already achieved what they envisioned, a crowded parking lot and a full house of worship. Today the Valley Family Church boasts a membership of well over 4,000 and the numbers continue to grow steadily. From conception comes birth.

During our interview, Beth Jones said, *"In my experience, there are essential elements that are necessary for effective leadership. One is vision, because the leader is the person who is out in front. As the leader, you are seeing things that other people aren't seeing. You are seeing beyond the horizon. You have to know where you are going and what the finish line looks like."* Beth Jones lives this belief. In fact, each of the women leaders in this book also held vision as number one on their list of leadership essentials.

Patricia Caruso's entire career, especially her rise from the position of a prison warden to director of the Michigan Department of Corrections, provides a model for the power of vision. She says, *"I'm a big picture thinker and I've always had a vision of where I want to go."* Patricia's greatest contribution was to take a distinctly different vision of a safer community and share it with stakeholders in ways that allowed them to actively participate in making it a reality. In Patricia's view, her role as the director was not just to keep the community safe by incarcerating criminals, but also by rehabilitating prisoners so that, after release, they could function in the world as safe and responsible citizens. This view is very different from the way prisons are normally perceived—as a way of protecting society by keeping criminals away from the rest of the law-abiding population.

While Patricia's vision helped reduce the high costs of prison operation by releasing more rehabilitated prisoners into the community, it also meant the closure of several prisons, which led to the loss of several thousand jobs. This was a tough decision to initiate, but Patricia was able to manage the transition by keeping her eyes fixed on her vision and communicating it to the right people, enabling her to get "buy in" from various stakeholders to make the changes she wanted to create.

Patricia stated in an article, *"In the end, there has to be balance. MDOC (Michigan Department of Corrections) has to fulfill its mission of protecting the public while being fiscally responsible to the citizens of Michigan. Finding and maintaining that balance is difficult, and there are always forces trying to upset the balance. To withstand them, the department must continually focus on its mission to provide the greatest amount of public protection while making the most efficient use of the state's resources."* [15] The core work of the leader involves continuous and consistent focus on her vision.

Visionary Thinking: A Core Skill

Having a vision means you are focused on something bigger than what you can accomplish alone. Your vision will include others. Your vision will add value to the lives of others, and it will allow them to accomplish personal objectives within your larger vision. You already know from experience that people (yourself included) want to be involved in a larger vision. Think about the times you *got on board* with someone else's vision once you discovered how and where you would fit into that picture and what you were able to achieve thanks to teamwork and united effort.

This is a pedestrian example, but maybe you can appreciate it, especially if your experience parallels mine. Growing up with seven brothers, football dominated our television screen on weekends. On almost any Sunday in December or January it was not uncommon to find our favorite team, the Green Bay Packers, playing in blizzard conditions. During every game, as the TV camera panned the stadium, we would see the inevitable diehard Packer fan, naked from the waist up, chest painted dark green, with a big "chunk of cheese" on his head, jumping and shouting wildly. I guarantee it wasn't because he wanted to be on TV or to risk frostbite. He simply wanted to be a part of something greater than himself—a small part of the famous "Packer Mystique."

Going to the Core: Sharing the Vision

We all know there's a difference between being a small part of something and being the one who is leading the charge. Even the most inspired vision, based on core values, won't get off the ground unless others believe in, and grasp the importance of, an idea, practice, or institutional change. You need to inform and enroll others in your vision by clearly explaining it and consistently inviting them to join in. The lesson from the lives of the women I interviewed is this: If you have a vision you are passionate about, be bold and share it. A powerful vision, once shared, gives the best leaders an ability to create a sense of intimacy with hundreds, thousands, or even millions of people. Shared vision, based on strong values, helps everyone lay aside personal agendas as they work to accomplish the larger vision. Put another way, picking up the visionary baton typically requires reaching inward, toward the core of our higher selves and "doing the right thing," especially when the going gets tough.

Vision is connected to purpose, making it a logical choice for people to follow a visionary leader. Buying in and sharing the vision gives meaning to the work they do. When a technician tightens those screws on a piece of equipment, she needs to know that she is not just turning a screw, but that she's securing a piece of the wing on the aircraft that will safely transport millions of people from one place to another. She is aware that the amount of pressure she exerts on that screw could mean the difference between life and death for passengers who fly on that aircraft. This imbues her daily effort with greater meaning and makes her aware of the importance of the work she does every day.

When people understand exactly how the quality of their own work ties in with the vision of the leader, they buy in to the effort and help achieve it. Mary Ellen Rodgers echoes this when she says, *"People want to follow someone with a vision; they want to understand how that vision relates to them personally, not just as part of an organization. When people believe that you are telling the truth—that what you believe is best for them and the broader organization—they are much more likely to sign on and work hard to achieve your vision."*

Communicating the vision becomes even more important in fast-paced or rapidly changing environments where people tend to lose focus on what they are doing and how it ties into the vision and mission of the organization. They begin asking themselves, *"Where are we headed now?"* When people hesitate or start asking questions, it's imperative that the leader reiterates the vision. There is no such thing as too much communication. Kathie VanderPloeg says, *"In business, things happen so fast, they change constantly and with great speed, and the only way to keep people moving together with you is by communicating what you are doing and where the organization is going. Leaders have to be in constant communication at every level of the organization. That is the way that you build the necessary trust."*

Role Modeling: Coming from Your Core

According to La June Tabron, role modeling is one of the best ways to communicate your vision. There is nothing more inspiring than a leader who walks the talk, who's every action and decision embodies her vision. When La June took on the position of Chief Executive Officer of the W. K. Kellogg Foundation, she had T-shirts made for everyone in the organization. The front of the shirt read, *"It's not about me and it's not about you."* On the back was printed, *"It's all about the children."* She did this because she knew that when leadership changes, people get insecure about their future and question their role and fit within the organization. Some of them start thinking, *"I need to secure my future here; maybe I'd better start serving who I think may be the new leader so I don't lose my job."* This kind of thinking can derail the organization and delay the work because people are orienting themselves to new or even bogus priorities that do not align with the organizational vision.

La June wanted to establish the vision from the beginning. Her message was clear: *We are here to serve children, and I want to establish right up front that you don't have to shift and serve me because I'm the new leader. Nor do I want you to be serving yourself. We have to be selfless and think about what's best for the children we serve.* Having T-shirts made for the executive staff was La June's way of reinforcing and communicating her vision. The effort was so successful that everyone in the organization wanted to wear the T-shirts. Eventually, she had those shirts made for office staff in Mexico and in Haiti as well, and the words got translated into Creole, Portuguese, and Spanish! Such is the power of role modeling a vision.

Mary Ellen Sheets has another way of role modeling her vision for her moving franchise—a vision that includes everyone working together in an environment of service, transparency, and honesty. She wanted her organization free from unhealthy internal competition between colleagues. Visioning a culture where openness reigned, and where everyone worked hard in the interest of achieving the organization's goals, she modeled these visionary aspects in her own work. From the get-go, she never hesitated to do the hard work herself, whether it involved driving a truck or doing the accounts. Her employees always knew how much profit was being made and what was being spent. When she created a franchise for her business, she brought the same system of transparency and hard work into the network.

Her franchise culture is such that all franchisees know exactly how much the other owners make. She says, *"Everything is open. This has created a lot of positive peer pressure within the franchise. Also, owners can contact each other and ask, 'Why are you making so much profit? How did you do it?' They can also learn by seeing what other owners are doing."* She goes on to say, *"This began early on, when I had only the moving company and was running it alone. I started sitting down with different employees and showing them our financials. They were shocked; they had thought I just kept all the money. They didn't have any idea of the rent, truck payments, and other expenses. Once they fully realized how the business ran, they wanted to help."*

A Personal Example: Role Modeling to the Core

From my perspective, role modeling is a powerful way to communicate your vision and ensure that it will be absorbed and supported by your team. This fact was brought home to me while attending the memorial service for my father-in-law, Ed Wieringa. He wanted no funeral, no flowers, and *"no preacher prayin' over me."* His family honored his wishes and yet the loving Spirit that binds us all together was clearly present in the room of nearly 300 people who came to celebrate the 97 years this special man lived on this earth.

My husband Bill delivered the eulogy, followed by comments from his eight siblings who, one-by-one, shared stories about their father and of growing up on the family dairy farm in Middleville, Michigan. I can honestly say that it was one of the most touching, poignant, powerful personal tributes I've witnessed in a long time.

As one after the other spoke of their father, Ed Wieringa's character and core values became clear. So did his vision for his children. His unshakeable love and commitment to Katie, his wife of 70 years, and to his nine children, 28 grandchildren, and 35 great-grandchildren was evident. His work ethic was unquestionable. His kind and non-judgmental disposition inspired us all. But my brother-in-law Nick, one of Ed's nine children, shared the one story that spoke volumes about the man. It was a lesson in real leadership. Here are Nick's words:

"This story took place when Dad was in his mid-70's. I told Dad that over by Wayland someone had cut down a willow tree and there was a sign in the yard saying, 'free wood.' I told Dad that I was going to go get it and asked if he'd like to ride along. Dad said he'd like that. He helped me load up my truck, and we brought it home and unloaded the wood. When we were finished, Dad told me to go get a rake and shovel. I asked him what he wanted that for. He replied that we were going back to Wayland to pick up the limbs and rake up the leaves and sawdust that was in left in the yard. He explained to me that you should always try to leave something better than you found it. I don't know of many people who would have done that."

Ed Wieringa did not leave riches or social status to his children, but he did make them heirs to a wealth of personal enrichment through role modeling. He was a subtle man. He never preached nor forced his ideas on anyone, even his own children. He simply taught by example the way he wanted them to live their lives. Perhaps that's why his vision lives on through his six sons and three daughters, all of whom turned out to be kind, loving, non-judgmental people with a strong work ethic who always leave whatever they touch better than the way they found it.

Vision Plus Strategy Equals Unstoppable

Great leaders share compelling visions and communicate in ways that inspire others to enthusiastically follow them. But a compelling shared vision is only the beginning. Our women leaders all spoke of vision in tandem with strategy. After all, a vision without a plan is nothing but a dream. Lillian Bauder puts it well when she says, *"After the vision, though, there has to be an understanding of execution, and this is something that very few leaders have. It is not that you have a master strategic plan that was followed for many decades, and then ended up on shelves. It is that you have to say, 'This is where we want to go and these are the broad courses we think we need to take to get there.' A vision combined with strategy helps people understand not just where they're going, but how they will get there."*

I recall a time when my assistant, Dawn, a video aficionado and the person who has recorded and edited most of my online educational videos, helped me put together a speaker demo video for meeting planners. She had not done anything like that before, but felt confident she could do the job and I thought so, too. Because speech venues, topics, and expectations are constantly changing, I didn't want to invest thousands of dollars in a video that would soon be outdated and need to be replaced rather quickly. So it seemed like a wise choice to have Dawn help me put together something affordable.

This was exciting. I had what I thought was a clear vision of what I wanted the video to look like and the impact it would make on my audience. We pulled out the latest couple of video programs I had recorded in front of client audiences and viewed them together. I pointed out various segments I thought we could use while sharing with her the importance of having some music to enhance the presentation and bring the whole thing together.

Dawn took what I had and put together what she thought would make a wonderful video, and then sent me the link for my approval before posting it *live* online. Viewing it, I felt irritated and let down. The finished product was nothing like what I thought we'd discussed. But I also knew I had no one to blame but myself. I simply had not taken the time to communicate my expectations to her in a way that allowed her to clearly understand what I was envisioning. So, we went back to the drawing board—with time, energy, and money wasted. So much for my "bargain" project.

I should have known better. Having worked with leaders as a consultant and executive coach over several decades, I know that having goals and a clear plan for achieving them is critical. Accepting responsibility for less than stellar results, I again sat down with Dawn, clearly explaining my vision. Together, we viewed samples of demos that more clearly reflected what I had in mind, and this time she had a chance to ask questions. We spent time planning and discussing the project, making it possible for us to consider other elements to be included (or not). We cleared up anything that seemed confusing or unclear to either of us, ending with the joy of knowing we were both in total agreement as to the end result.

Two days later Dawn sent me another link. This time it did not disappoint. In fact, we were thrilled! Why? Because we had taken the time to thoroughly explore, discuss, and validate expectations, ask and answer questions, and negotiate specifics with one another. This time I did not assume that my expectations were clear. This time, together we created a product supported by a well-planned strategy that helped achieve my original vision of the project.

Vision is "What," Strategy is "How"

According to La June Tabron, setting a clear strategy allows people to understand exactly *how* they are expected to contribute toward making the vision a reality. Clear and cogent strategies set the pathways and parameters within which people can operate. This is important because without clear plans or boundaries, organizations lapse into the chaos of resistance, false starts, confusion, and even resentment. A cogent strategy enables people to understand what they should be doing and what they should *not* be doing. Decisions become easier to make when people ask themselves whether or not the actions they are about to take will complement the accepted strategy and work toward achieving the goal.

While no one wants to feel handcuffed by rigid rules, there's still a need for working within clear parameters. La June says, *"Having no clear rules and no boundaries can lead to unhealthy competition, positioning, and needless stress. I think a little bit of guidance, direction, and vision take that same energy and allow people to be more grounded in where they are going. And I see that people thrive much better in that kind of an environment."*

Having a clear plan and strategy is one thing, but execution of the strategy is quite another. Executing the strategy can be a tough job, requiring ongoing monitoring and follow up. During the execution of strategy, a leader may need to make a series of tough calls in the interest of the organization's welfare. Talk about core work! As our featured women leaders found, their decisions have had direct influence on the lives of their people as well as their organizations. Again and again, their stories confirm that a leader must be decisive, even in situations where an unpopular decision is necessary. As Lillian Bauder puts it, *"Some people love what you do and some hate what you do, particularly when tough decisions are made for the best of the corporation. For that reason, good leadership takes courage."* Cheryle Touchton agrees, *"Leaders can't worry about whether other people are going to be happy with them or mad at them. They need to have the courage to do the right thing. And it does take courage to do the right thing in the face of adversity or when some people would like you to do something different."*

Clear Vision Makes Easier Decisions

Reaching into your core and making tough decisions doesn't come easily to everyone. If you are an approval seeking person who wants everybody to be happy and to like you, leadership is going to be a tough row to hoe. This is where, not just knowing your strengths, but being able to pinpoint and monitor areas that need development comes into play. You might need to strengthen your inner discipline and exterior bearing so you quit throwing those "gutter balls" as Beth Jones once did just to stay on someone's good side. Leaders need to be strong and courageous. They know how to confine their emotions so they are able to do the right thing and make the right decision, even if it's initially unpopular. As Touchton says, *"Managing emotions is key to being an effective leader."*

Kathie VanderPloeg learned this lesson the hard way. In the beginning of her leadership journey, she wanted to be the kind of leader that everybody loved. But then she realized that her desire to be liked often conflicted with making decisions that were best for the business and for the people whose livelihoods depended on the company being successful.

197

She says, *"I thought that I could make everyone like me, and I had to learn that that is not going to happen. Leaders have to make difficult decisions, they have to do things that people don't always appreciate, and, in a lot of cases, the leader's decisions have an impact on people's futures."*

Gail McGovern realized that decisions become easier when you keep the vision in mind. Her advice to emerging leaders is to train oneself to make every decision based on whether or not it's good for the business. Every time you are confused as to what decision to make, Gail recommends checking back to the vision rather than what the boss or the team wants. She says, *"If you are making fact-based decisions, based on what is best for your company or your organization, your motives are clear, and I believe you will likely make fewer mistakes."*

Making tough decisions on strategies connected to fulfilling the vision is an essential part of a leader's core work. Some people call this the "loneliness" of leadership. In the short run, you may make a few enemies. But if you have a clear and well-articulated vision for your organization or team, if you communicate it frequently, and execute your strategy efficiently and effectively, in the end, those who don't buy in will either eventually fall into step or find a way out. The good news in this seemingly bad news is that you'll end up with a team that not only gets on board with your vision, but one that is also motivated to help you achieve it.

CHAPTER 11

CRAFT A 3-C TEAM

"Surround yourself with a trusted and loyal team.
It makes all the difference." —Alison Pincus

Although leaders sometimes feel alone, they don't lead alone. They don't work alone. True leadership requires a team, and an inspired one at that; a team that's willing to get in line, reach into their core, and do what needs to be done. Football coaches often use a phrase that serves as an analogy to inspire their teams: *Hold the rope!* Keeping the phrase *hold the rope* in mind, here is a classic exercise to try. Imagine you're hanging from a cliff with a 10,000-foot drop below. The only thing holding you to that cliff is a rope—and that rope is being held by someone.

Here's the point: If you had a choice, who would be holding that rope for you? Who in your organization would you trust to hold on to that rope for as long as necessary? Who would be willing to struggle with all their might, to bloody their hands if needed, because they would never, ever let go of you? Are you thinking of only one person? Maybe two? What if you had an entire team who would hold onto that rope for you? What would it take to accomplish that?

I ask you to consider this for one reason: No leader becomes unstoppable without an entire team willing to *hold the rope* for whomever may be in need. This is the kind of support it takes to move the team toward the leader's vision for the organization. High achieving leaders know that to accomplish something great, they need a core team of people who are committed and courageous, who can and will compensate for the leader's deficiencies, and who get along so well that they openly rely on each other. They are a team of people willing to *hold the rope*.

During my interviews I found differences among our women leaders in terms of the subjects they chose to focus on or explain in detail. But a tie that bound them together was the belief that they could not have achieved their success without a trustworthy team who supported them and each other. They all considered this kind of teamwork a critical component of their success. Each leader has put her belief into action by hiring a team she believes has the right attitude and the right competencies to put their strategies into action. Martha Mertz, for example, says, *"The other thing I did to keep growing was to attract the kind of people who have become part of the ATHENA family, people who have helped move the organization forward. They helped find the resources, the funding and the people to carry it on, to make it grow and expand beyond the original vision. If we hadn't been able to attract such utterly outstanding people along the way, ATHENA wouldn't have been able to happen in the way it has."*

Gail McGovern took on the role as head of the toll-free numbers business at AT&T at a time when 800 phone numbers were going portable. She knew she was taking on a job no one else wanted. Toll free numbers had never been portable, and AT&T had the largest market share of the 800 business. Portability would hit their business hard. But Gail was confident in her own abilities and in what she calls an *"extraordinary team."* Within eighteen months, Gail and her team revamped the entire business from advertising, sales strategy, to customer service and more. Ultimately, instead of an expected ten-point loss in business, AT&T lost only two points of the market share. Gail says, *"I had an incredible team. We loved working together. We were too naive to know we'd signed on for an impossible task and the outcome was stunning."*

No wonder Gail McGovern believes that hiring the right people is the most important task of the leader. She knows from experience that the right people in the right roles at the right time can mean the difference between incredible success and devastating defeat, especially when the stakes are high. She says, *"I believe that the most important decisions you make are in choosing the people that you surround yourself with."*

It's not a surprise that Steve Jobs was known to hire only A+ people to work at Apple. In 1999, he told Time magazine, *"My #1 job here at Apple is to make sure that the top 100 people are A+ players. And everything else will take care of itself. If the top 50 people are right, it just cascades down throughout the whole organization."* [16]

Enter the 3-C Team

While exploring the team aspect of leadership, I was curious to know what kind of people our women leaders chose to surround themselves with. Did they focus purely on competence? Was it experience they were looking for? What sort of skills did they hire for? It was an interesting question and the answers were quite surprising. Obviously, they all hired for competence, a fundamental requirement for any job. But competence aside, they gave immense importance to three core qualities they looked for in a candidate. These were the traits they sought before even considering someone for their "inner team." These were the individuals they would rely on for support in executing the strategy that would accomplish the vision and mission of their organizations. Here is the 3-C formula our leaders sought when hiring, and they settled for nothing less: Courage, Complementary strengths, and Chemistry.

Courage

We all admire the virtue of courage, especially in others. Sometimes we don't see it so much in ourselves. Courage isn't always heroic, sometimes it's one simple, honest, straightforward act, and as La June Tabron would say, *"Just the right thing to do."*

I witnessed this trait in my son, Joey, when he was just a seventh grader. He and I were on our way to a local restaurant for a quick meal. Getting out of the car, he said to me, *"Hey, Mom, I did something today that was really difficult."*

"And what was that, Joey?"

"I told a girl that I wasn't interested in her."

"You told a girl you weren't interested in her?"

"Yeah. She's liked me for a couple of weeks now, but I'm not really interested in her—at least, not as a girlfriend."

"How did she take it?"

"She was a little embarrassed."

"How do you know that?"

"Well, she told me that it kind of embarrassed her. I did tell her that I liked her as a friend, but she didn't say much to that."

"How did you feel once you'd told her?

"Much better. It was a relief just telling her the truth. Now, I guess I

know what is meant by 'the truth will set you free,' because I sure feel a lot freer—like a weight is off my shoulders."

"Good. I'm glad you feel freer. I'm proud of you for having the courage to tell her."

"Yeah, me, too."

In the larger scheme of things, this was a simple incident—a brief conversation—a discovered *truth*. This moment of courage elevated Joey's self-esteem and expanded his heart. For him, it was a lesson in the power of honesty.

This story explains what I mean by the word *courage* in the context of crafting a 3-C team. Some leaders make the mistake of surrounding themselves with *yes* people who tell them what they want to hear; people who, like the Processionary Caterpillar, follow along, no matter what. Some organizations encourage managers to recruit candidates with no history of confrontation in their prior jobs, thinking they are screening out troublemakers, but as you can imagine, that opens up all kinds of possible pitfalls.

Some organizations do not want, nor do they support, the courageous act of constructive disagreement, but this is death to a team. As a consequence, leaders and managers in these "protective" cultures are not skilled in managing conflict or receiving constructive feedback. They feel threatened when someone on their team points out their mistakes, finds gaps in their strategy, or challenges the status quo. As a result, even the most honest people find themselves keeping their mouths shut for fear of reprisal.

Courage to the Core

However, truly great leaders know the secret to forming the perfect team: they seek out people who have the *courage* to speak the truth regardless of the consequences. Truly great leaders create an environment where the truth can be spoken, where people feel confident that their honest opinions and feedback will be seriously considered and respected.

La June believes in creating a culture of openness in the organization where people feel free to voice their objections. She also believes it's important to surround herself with honest people who will tell her the truth. According to La June, *"When you move away from your family, you have to find people who will tell you the truth, who will expect more from you no matter what you're doing, and then give you some good advice, or at least another perspective."* The world's most successful leaders know that without honest feedback, a leader cannot survive.

Steve Jobs, for instance, would routinely take his top 100 employees on an annual retreat where he would present his strategy for the coming year and solicit their feedback and suggestions. Though famous (or perhaps infamous) for being temperamental, Jobs was always open to argument and feedback from his designers.

Bill Gates, too, is known for encouraging people to speak up. Satya Nadella, the new CEO of Microsoft, has this to say about Bill Gates: *"You can push back on him. He'll argue with you vigorously for a couple of minutes, and then he'll be the first person to say, 'Oh, you're right.'"* [11]

While it takes courage to speak up, hearing and accepting the truth calls for a lot of courage on the part of the leader, too. Leaders who lack confidence in their capabilities fear feedback, and, as a consequence, they fail to flourish. And yes, accepting feedback is hard. It's tempting to become a dictator when you are at the top, to reject honesty with an *off with your head* retort. It's the psychologically strong leader who can look at feedback objectively and analyze whether it's worth keeping or not, without wanting to fire the person who said it. Mary Ellen Rodgers says, *"You have to make yourself somewhat vulnerable with your team, particularly for those who report directly to you, so they will believe that they can give you honest feedback without reprisal."*

You probably sense that courage is as much about the leader as it is about the team. The leader has to have courage to listen to bad news, and team members need courage to convey it. Kathie VanderPloeg says, *"People who are working for you need to feel that they can tell you what is happening. I always tell people that I don't like surprises and that it is okay to make mistakes—there is no retribution for making mistakes. It's the only way that we really advance and grow. I need to hear the bad news as well as the good news. The only way we can solve problems or improve is by our employees telling us what our issues are."*

Why is it so important for leaders to have team members who are willing to tell them the truth? Because without honest feedback or gentle challenges, leaders can be susceptible to *hubris*, thinking their way is the only way. It can be tempting to reject or deny constructive criticism or negative feedback. Leadership has its hard moments; there are many roles to fill, many moments of firefighting issues that pop up at the most inconvenient times. Leaders often have to make quick decisions, sometimes without sufficient information because time is of the essence. And they do all this and more in full public view. Leaders know that every move and every decision they make will be scrutinized, analyzed, and criticized. Having to accept constructive feedback is difficult, because a leader's failures are painfully visible for the world to see.

According to Lillian Bauder, when you become the leader, people want to please you. It's a natural instinct to stay on the good side of one's boss. This means even though you emphasize your desire for openness and honesty, there may always be people who tell you what they think you want to hear, rather than what really needs to be said. This is why successful leaders screen out those kinds of people. Ruth Shaw counsels, *"Run from people who aren't trustworthy, people you can't count on to tell you the truth."*

Unfortunately, we've seen leaders who willingly surround themselves with people who affirm their decisions. They are unwilling to hold up and face the mirror of truth. Such leaders may become powerful in the short run, but their success is unsustainable. At their worst, such leaders can cause the demise of their organizations. Think about Enron and Arthur Anderson for example.

Leaders who become those others wish to emulate not only allow feedback, they actively encourage their team members to speak that truth. This is why when they hire and select their team members, they choose people who possess the inherent courage to speak the truth.

Complementary Strengths

It is said that strong leaders surround themselves with strong people. However, after interviewing so many strong women leaders, I realized that strong leaders actually surround themselves with people who are in fact *stronger than themselves* in areas where the leader herself might lack some specific skills. I use the word "complementary" to describe how strong leaders hire for abilities that complete the skill set of their innermost teams.

As we know, the word "complementary" means *"completing something else or making it better; going together well: working well together."*[18]

When selecting their teams, our twelve leaders have often chosen those who complemented their own skills, or who could cover for the leader's own deficiencies.

Kathie VanderPloeg says, *"The best decisions I have ever made were to hire managers for the organization who have skills that I don't and who are better than I am."*

Ruth Shaw says, *"I looked for people who were, in one way or another, stronger or better than I was—people from whom I could learn....I tried to work at complementary skills sets."*

Mary Ellen Rodgers says, *"Quite frankly, what you need to do is to bolster your own strengths and weaknesses, and then look to people to fill the holes around you."*

Naomi Rhode found an interesting way to hire the person who best complemented her strengths. She talks about the time when she was the president of the National Speaker's Association and had to select a chairperson who would be in charge of all of the meetings that year, including the national convention, winter workshops, and learning labs. Naomi selected ten potential candidates for the job, and then consulted with her husband about choosing criteria for identifying the right person. Her husband suggested that she create a graph with a scale from one to ten, putting herself in the middle of the scale and then plotting all ten candidates on that graph. Those she considered stronger than herself would get points higher than she would give herself.

Naomi says, *"It helped me understand that I wanted someone stronger than I was. I wanted people who were the very best; I chose those kinds of people, and I was not wrong. Because I chose such stellar people, they kept amazing me with what they did."*

I know from my own experience of attending several meetings before, during, and after Naomi's presidency, that the National Speaker's Association enjoyed some of the best conferences and workshops during her tenure. The risks in programming that were taken that year paid off in spades. The selection of presenters was top notch, and the entertainment provided was like nothing NSA members had experienced ever before. Absolutely everything was done at the height of excellence. Naomi and her team raised the bar for future conferences.

Hiring or selecting people stronger or more skilled than you in the areas that complement your respective strengths and offset your weaknesses makes a lot of sense. After all, on a personal level, if you didn't know much about finance, you'd probably hire a good accountant. The same goes for effective leaders. They fill in the gaps. They create a team that's skilled and competent, whole in every way. You'd think everyone would do that, wouldn't you? Unfortunately, that's not always the case. Many leaders choose to surround themselves with people less talented than themselves out of fear of being overshadowed by a member of their team. Rather than recognizing their responsibility as a leader to hire the right people to do the work with excellence, they renege on their duty. But great leaders hire and value team players with complementary skills and competencies.

Chemistry

It seems clear at this point that neither blind "get in line followers" nor "better than average" employees will take an organization where the leader wants to go. But, contrary to what is commonly believed, it isn't always the smartest, most talented people who will, either. Take one of my former clients for example, a large paperboard packaging company who hired a brilliant, talented, and highly educated man as their senior engineer. They were thrilled to snag this guy, beating out the competition—or so they thought. Lou hadn't been with them long before they realized their mistake. Lou turned out to be aloof and self-absorbed, holding most people and their ideas in disdain. There had been hopes that Lou would manage the department when the current manager retired, but leaders quickly realized that the chemistry between Lou and his teammates was simply not a good fit for their organization. He was there less than a year when they let him go.

Several of our twelve unstoppable leaders mentioned the importance of hiring candidates based on chemistry—how well they would fit in with other team members and the leader's style of running things. Some of our leaders actually used the word "chemistry" to describe what they meant while others used the term "collaboration," or the phrase, "a good fit."

Gail McGovern, for example, says, *"When I talk about staffing for chemistry, I don't mean you should bring in a bunch of people who think like you do. You may get along, but you will march right off a cliff together if there is no one to bounce off interesting and different kinds of ideas."* She goes on to say that when she hires people, she often has the rest of the team interview the candidate as well, and if they don't get along well, she just won't hire the person. There simply needs to be a good *fit*.

Beth Jones defines "chemistry" as *gelling* together, or getting along well. She says, *"Great leaders have talked about what they have looked for in team building, and we have adopted many of these principles. First of all, do we click with the people who are going to be on our leadership team or in our ministry? Chemistry is important."*

When there's chemistry between team members, or "clickage," as I like to call it, it's so much easier to create a team that's on fire. When you have highly motivated individuals willing to bring their total selves to the game and collaborate in ways that move the team forward with energy and optimism, you've got chemistry.

Getting the Right Mix

Creating chemistry depends not just on the team the leader assembles, but on the leader, as well. Once she selects the right people, she sets the tone for the team. A lackluster leader will create a lackluster team. An energized, motivated, passionate leader, afire with the vision, will create a team with those qualities. She will naturally weed out the negative and untrustworthy people from her team (if any exist) and hire only those who have a similar passion.

This topic makes me think about the board game "Cranium" and its founders, Richard Tait and Whit Alexander. Cranium, an award-winning board game, is one of the best-selling independent board games in U.S. history. Founded by two young Microsoft alumni, their company culture focuses on creating products that are Clever, High quality, Innovative, Friendly, and Fun (CHIFF). Anything that is not CHIFF—including letterheads, logo, product innovations, even meetings, is unacceptable at Cranium. With such passionate and motivated leaders at the helm, it's no surprise that the people who work at Cranium are also CHIFF and enjoy a great mix of chemistry.

Crafting a 3-C team is a challenge, but it's worth the effort. As Gail McGovern says, *"If I were asked to say, in one word, the most important thing for a leader to focus on, it would be 'staffing.' I believe that as you progress in an organization, the most important decisions that you make are in choosing the team of people that you surround yourself with."* Gail then went on to talk about a time she hired a nanny for her daughter. Her husband lined up the candidates and she did the interviewing. After 18 hours of interviews, rejecting the majority of the 35 he'd identified, Gail finally found a finalist.

While the woman was spending two full days with Gail's daughter, Gail interviewed every reference and even some the candidate hadn't provided. Gail's husband commented that if she did that kind of scrutinizing of potential hires at work she'd not get anything done. To which she replied, *"This is exactly what I do at work."* The nanny was with for them for six years and Gail credits that woman for their daughter turning out so well. Like hiring in the workplace, when you do the hard work up front, when you take the time to truly craft your team, you end up with the right people who are ready and willing to serve.

I used the term *craft* because it infers *intentionality* about who you hire, that you carefully select the right people even if it takes a long time to assemble the right mix. As Gail McGovern says, *"I have learned the hard way that if you just staff for expediency, you will regret it. You should limp along with a vacancy rather than staff just for expediency."*

A 3-C team takes time to craft, and it pays high dividends. All members are competent to the core—that is the fundamental aspect of a good mix. Competent team members bring strength where the leader may need the advantage of a particular skill, knowledge base, or expertise. They are courageous and honest, and, as a leader, you should expect them to tell you the truth and give you critical feedback. You should be able to count on them to point out mistakes, challenge you, or pick holes in your strategy. Crafting a C-3 team means everyone supports your vision and is one hundred percent committed to the goals, yet when things go off track, you can expect pushback because you're all there to advance the organization. To encourage the spirit of collaboration, leaders create an environment where people feel supported, encouraged, and motivated to perform at their best.

Lillian Bauder sums it up well when she says, *"Part of my biggest challenge was both getting people who were excellent and then getting people who were excellent who also could participate in a team."* It begins with you, your transparency, and the level of trust you create by being honest and upfront with people. It ends with the core chemistry that binds your team together so you can achieve successful results.

CHAPTER 12

CULTIVATE

CRITICAL RELATIONSHIPS

"True leaders understand that leadership is not about them but about those they serve. It is not about exalting themselves but about lifting others up." –Sheri L. Dew

Ralph, a psychologist friend of mine, agreed to help me dig for more of my own personal stories that I could use in my presentations and training sessions. Not only do these personal stories help me to create connections with my audiences, but, if told well, they make my message memorable.

Ralph asked me, *"What was it like for you growing up? What fun, exciting things happened that you can recall?"* I could remember plenty of wonderful memories as a small child, but as I grew older, I honestly couldn't remember having a lot of fun. I wasn't allowed to go places with friends when it was for the sole purpose of having fun. My overly protective father wanted to keep his kids safe, and, I believe, he felt that the best way to protect us was to keep us at home. Outside of school-sponsored events, I was rarely allowed to go places. For example, after a football game when the other kids would head to Hansen's Drive-In to congregate and hang out, I was expected to head home.

Ralph asked, *"How did that make you feel?"* That was an easy one to answer. *"Lonely. Isolated. Sad. As much as my father loved us, he seemed more concerned with our safety than with what we thought about our lives or how we felt. I was just a kid; what did I know?"* As wonderful as my family was, a lack of real dialogue made fertile ground for creating feelings of disconnection or alienation. I tell you this because far too many people in organizations today experience a similar sense of not being truly connected to what's going on.

People struggle desperately to build teams, to engage their employees, and to gain loyalty and commitment. Why? Because they don't know how to genuinely connect with those they need a relationship with in order to form the team, get the commitment, or achieve personal or organizational goals.

On the other hand, leaders who achieve high levels of success for themselves, those who are able to lead their organizations forward to the accomplishment of their mission and vision, are adept at cultivating relationships through excellent communication skills and nurturing behaviors. They connect vigilantly with people both inside and outside the organization. They form deep and supportive connections with their own families, and they often treat their employees with the same sensitivity and caring they would show family members.

These leaders intentionally build strong connections with all kinds of people, showing a genuine concern for those who work for them and with them, getting to know people at every level in the organization. In fact, the importance of relationship building appears to be an ingrained mindset of great leaders, regardless of their personal leadership style. They just genuinely care about people. For example, Gail McGovern says, *"I truly do care about the people I work with. I am the kind of person that likes establishing human connection. I am innately curious about human beings and their lives, and I try to connect in a very personal way, instead of just being concerned about their professional lives."* Cheryle Touchton wholeheartedly agrees. She says, *"Relationships are everything, they are truly everything. In order to develop a relationship, you have to honestly care for the person."*

Every one of the leaders I interviewed for this book spoke about relationship building as being critical to their success. Patricia Caruso speaks about her time as a warden of a large prison. Despite being in charge of so many people, she found the time to develop close personal relationships with them. Despite the fact that she was responsible for more than 2000 prisoners and 700 staff, she made it a point to know her people and the prisoners she managed.

In fact, Patricia felt energized to be with the people who worked for

her and with her. According to her, the best days of her work life as director of the Department of Corrections are those that she spent out in the
field rather than in the office. She developed great relationships with her
colleagues and especially with the employee union. Patricia said that so
much more was accomplished because she enjoyed good relationships.

Patricia had a really difficult mission to accomplish: changing the
mindset from *"keeping communities safe by incarcerating criminals indef-
initely"* to *"keeping communities safer by rehabilitating prisoners so that
they don't commit any more crimes."* In order to realize this mission, she
needed the buy-in at every level. Cultivating relationships with staff, unions,
prisoners, and leaders was imperative. It's obvious that developing strong
relationships was critical to Patricia's success as director of the Michigan
Department of Corrections. However, that was not the sole driver of her
desire to connect. As a leader, she operated out of a sense of deep compassion for her staff as well as the prisoners. This genuine "people sense"
is what helped her rise to the position of director.

Other leaders too have demonstrated a similar innate desire to connect with people. While setting up ATHENA International, Martha Mertz
had to make an enormous number of calls to connect with people. She
had to do this in order to identify the people needed to build a network.
Sometimes, she would call an office to talk to a senior professional and a
secretary or receptionist would pick up the phone. Martha realized that it
was an opportunity for her to build a relationship with this person who
oftentimes would be the gatekeeper. But her interest went deeper than
that. Martha genuinely cared about people, and she loved discovering
their stories. She says, *"I figured out later that it was probably the best
thing I could have done. It wasn't about what it could do for me. I genuinely cared about this voice on the other end of the line who was always
there and who served a very good purpose, but who often wasn't noticed
by very many people."*

It is not hard to create deep bonds with people if you're willing to do
the little things that demonstrate genuine caring. Kathie VanderPloeg and
Mary Ellen Sheets make it a point to know the names of their employees
and their families. They bring them small gifts and ask about their children.
Lillian Bauder does the same. Though it may seem like a little thing to do,
it demonstrates a leader's caring respect, something extremely important

to people who want to know that they are seen as a human being first and foremost. Mary Ellen Rodgers takes every call with a remote employee as an opportunity to ask them about a challenge that they're facing at work, and offers them some advice on how to handle it. All these strong, active, busy women have somehow found the time to create great relationships all around them.

Connecting with people takes time and effort, and is something you need to be conscious about doing. Obstacles such as time and distance never got in the way of our twelve women leaders building deep and lasting connections with people. When Naomi Rhode was president of the National Speakers Association, and later when she led the Global Federation of Speakers, she made it a point to meet with the board of directors of all the chapters that made up each of the organizations, even though it was not a requirement of her position, and she did this at her own expense. She says, *"Now, is that something I should be applauded for? Maybe—but it was very self-serving because as I went to every chapter, as I met with all of those chapter boards, and all of the boards of those other countries, I got to know people eyeball-to-eyeball. Then I wasn't so remote because they knew me."*

Connection Conquers Distance

The Unstoppables dispel the notion that geographical distance is an obstacle in creating and sustaining deep rewarding connections with people. According to them, if you have a genuine intention to cultivate a relationship, you can always find a means to do so. For example, right after Mary Ellen Rodgers took over her role as Deloitte LLP's U.S. Managing Partner for Workplace Services, the company put a ban on travel because of the economic downturn. Mary Ellen's direct reports, however, were based all across the country, with some as far away as India. This meant that she had to find a way to connect with all of these people personally over the Internet and phone.

She told me during the interview that she needed to get really creative with media because it is so easy to lose the personal touch over the phone or in email or Skype. She says, *"Since I believe that creating connective tissue is so important in a well-functioning team, I really needed to look for opportunities, cues, and small signs on how to connect. I had to find out what was important to the people on my team, and to remember to relate to them through things like instant messenger.*" She would take every opportunity to meet people directly, and if she ever travelled, she would find the time to have personal discussions with people apart from the required work-related discussions.

Cultivating critical relationships necessitates a genuine fondness for people. You need to *want* to connect with people, not because you want something from others, but because you want to give them something— your time, interest, and genuine attachment. If you're not the sort of leader who has an innate desire to connect with people, it will be more difficult for you to cultivate enduring relationships, but it's still possible. It will involve stepping out of your comfort zone to get connected, if only with your inner team. For example, Steve Jobs often delegated "people management" to his core team because he was not the sort of person who could connect deeply with everybody in ways that were obvious. Despite this, his team absolutely adored him and considered themselves lucky for having worked with him. Clearly, he did connect with them at some level, even though he could come across as abrasive or aloof.

Some of our leaders talked about the importance of being politically astute as a requirement to developing relationships, not just with their supporters but also with those who are in opposition to them. From Abraham Lincoln to Golda Meir, from Winston Churchill to Indira Gandhi, leaders who have achieved notable success have known how to handle their critics and enemies. It's very possible that not everyone will want you to succeed. The successful leaders are the ones that build a broad base of support and work their networks when needed. Lillian Bauder explains it this way: "*You may get most people on your side, but not everybody wants you to succeed. So you need to know how to talk to people who are in opposition to you. How do you handle that one person on your board that always has to publicly disagree with you? You have a private meeting with that person ahead of time, so you find out that person's concerns and deflect the public criticism and on, and on, and on. There is a political astuteness that is absolutely critical in a very, very effective leader.*"

In my book, *You CAN Teach a Pig to Sing – Create Great Relationships… with Anyone, Anytime, Anywhere,* I offer a number of strategies for creating critical relationships, including those with whom you struggle to connect and communicate—strategies that all great leaders have taken the time to cultivate. In every leadership seminar, I ask people to describe the traits of the best leader they have ever had the honor of working for, and then to describe the worst person for whom they've ever worked. Without exception, the trait that comes to the top of the list of traits of exceptional leaders is the *ability to listen*. The trait that comes to the top of the worst leaders is the *inability to listen*. Cheryle Touchton commented repeatedly on the importance of listening—to employees, customers, everyone. In fact, when you read the profiles of all our special leaders in this book, you will find over and over again that genuinely caring for people has been key to their achieving success—a caring that has been demonstrated in any number of ways, most of which involve listening, sharing openly, and taking time to learn about their team members' interests and likes.

Taking Time to Care

It makes a difference to people when a leader knows what's going on with employees' families, even to knowing names of children or spouses; giving gifts for birthdays, weddings, or anniversaries to expressing sympathy after a loss. Our leaders know the value of spending time in conversation to understand the concerns and challenges or ideas of employees, and keeping people informed. A leader's ability to listen with an open mind and heart helps create relationships that are not only meaningful to those the leader serves, but meaningful to the leader herself who is rewarded in ways unimagined.

Lillian Bauder, while president and CEO at Cranbrook Educational Community, developed such a close relationship with members of the AFSCME Union (a union she described as "really tough"), garnering so much love and commitment from them, that when she left Cranbrook, the members of the union went above and beyond. As she said, *"They had a picnic for me, gave me an AFSCME T-shirt, flowers, and then very importantly, they went up the hierarchy and got a steward badge for me, saying that every union needs a great steward and I had been Cranbrook's great steward. I still have that badge."*

La June Tabron tells a story of a time when she didn't feel heard or respected, a story that she often shares with those in her organization because, as she says, *"It lets others know how I felt about not being heard, and how I felt when I wasn't even consulted, and how I felt when I wasn't trusted, but how I turned all that around by staying and helping build a platform so that others can feel more heard and respected. I don't preach to people."* It is through her sharing openly, including her own mistakes, that she builds relationships and, at the same time, models the value of *connecting* with others that she holds so dear.

Gail McGovern is such a people-person that her husband teases her constantly, saying things like, *"You are the only person I know who can take a five-minute cab ride and know where the taxi driver is from, how many kids they have."* She readily admits to being innately curious about human beings and their lives. *"I try to connect in a very personal way, instead of just being concerned about their professional lives."* As the CEO, Gail is aware that there is a difference between demonstrating genuine care for the people who work for her or with her and becoming close friends.

While Gail has always believed it is important for people to have close friends at work, she does say, *"The thing that is tricky about being the president and CEO is that it is kind of hard to let your hair down. It is not like I don't trust the people I work with; I adore them, but they don't necessarily want to see me sweat. This is the type of position where you are a little bit more in a fishbowl or under the microscope and, therefore, you have to find your sources of support in other places."* Gail went on to talk about the importance of finding CEO's from other organizations, or leaders on other boards on which she has served, to give her advice and counsel—and the importance of nurturing these relationships as well. And, of course, many of our leaders spoke about the importance of having a strong supportive relationship at home with their spouse where they could share openly their most personal concerns with no worries or repercussions.

The core work of a leader involves crafting a compelling vision and engaging people in that vision. It calls on the leader to craft a 3-C team where people have the courage to speak the truth, where team members are selected for their competence and for chemistry—being a good *fit* with the rest of the team. And the core work of a leader also involves genuinely caring for those the leader serves. To do this work you may need to step out of your comfort zone to extend your reach as some of our leaders have done. This work calls on you to be intentional, and though it may be difficult to do, it is possible when you're committed to do the work demanded of you to succeed. The twelve unstoppable leaders have demonstrated such a commitment, and, as a result, with the help of all those they serve, they have had the honor of making a tangible contribution to their organizations, their communities, and to the world.

As a bonus for this book, you can get your very own My Unstoppable Career Fast Track Guide at **www.MyUnstoppableCareer.com**

CONTRIBUTION

The Three Ls of Contribution:

LEAD

a Life of Service

LEAVE

a Lasting Legacy

LOOK

After What's Been Entrusted to You

CHAPTER 13

CONTRIBUTION: THE FOURTH LEADERSHIP CORNERSTONE

"The human contribution is the essential ingredient.
It is only in the giving of oneself to others that
we truly live." –Ethel Percy Andrus

I t comes as no surprise that leaders who make it to the pinnacle possess a variety of admirable traits and numerous capabilities that keep them at the top of their game. The unstoppable leader possesses strength of character; she is internally aligned, resilient, and has an unquenchable spirit that shows up in self-confidence and fortitude. She is a visionary, able to imbue her team with trust built on her own firm commitment to follow her passion, fulfill on her promises, and do what she says she will do. She forges ahead with fortitude when the circumstances seem daunting and the work difficult.

She learns from her mistakes, strives for excellence in her relationships, and models that which she wants or expects from others. She learns, not just from books or formal education, but from experience, personal reflection, and affiliation in professional associations. She gains a lifetime of knowledge and wisdom from people and in places where others may least expect it or would think to look. Underlying everything is an inner drive to lead a life of service, to *contribute* where and when she can. And it is her *contribution* that will ultimately define her.

In reviewing the stories of our unstoppable leaders who reached the top, I am impressed by their contributions in creating transformation, advancing new systems, developing their people, building sustainable growth, and making a lasting difference. In addition to career growth and achievement, I am impressed by the seemingly small but significant contributions to the lives of others, both inside and outside their organizations. Case in point, the thank-you notes, personal visits, listening ears, small gifts, personal inquiries, and all the time spent in getting to know employees and remain connected with stakeholders.

The Components of Contribution

I found myself wondering how these busy, successful women, from CEOs, presidents, and senior leaders to owners of businesses and large franchises, find the time to do all that they do for others while leading teams, running their organizations, making life-altering decisions, and managing untold numbers of people. I've come to the conclusion that these women have the ability to draw others into their visions, while, at the same time, stay firmly grounded in the *present*. I get the sense that they're constantly asking themselves, *"How can I best handle this event, work with this person, deal with this issue in this moment? How can I contribute to this person's life right now?"* I've also come to believe that it is their ability to be in the *present moment,* while keeping their eye on the big picture, that allows them to find the time and the resources to serve their employees in such a personal manner. This seems to be what differentiates the high achieving, inspiring leaders from the merely "successful" ones.

Patricia Caruso chose to personally inform her Corrections staff when the prison was being shut down. Martha Mertz took the time to personally connect with every receptionist or secretary who took her call. Naomi Rhode used her own time and money to travel around the world to meet face-to-face with her association members. La June Tabron takes the time to discover the story behind the story. All of our leaders display a genuine desire to serve, to give something of themselves to the people with whom they interact. Their countless lasting contributions set them apart from so-called average or merely "good" leaders.

It is the gift of contribution for which our twelve leaders will be remembered: the love they shared, the helping hand they offered, the positive moments they created with individuals at every level, and the changes they made both inside the organization and outside, as well. *This* is the legacy that will remain after they're gone and life has moved on. These are the stories that will be passed from generation to generation, serving as ongoing inspiration to those who follow.

Contribution Equals Caring

When I think of contribution, a name immediately comes to mind—one not associated with business, salaries, organizational titles, political movements, or social causes. The name I associate with the word "contribution" is Mother (my own).

My mother was my greatest role model, and, to this day, the one I most desire to emulate. Although she never would have considered herself a *leader*, others did. My mother, Mabel Marian Nolan, would have told you that the only reason she ended up on the board in any of the many volunteer organizations she belonged to was because someone needed to fill the role. And because she lived to serve, she was a natural. People were constantly turning to my mother for advice, *"Mabel, what would you do?" "Mabel, what do you think?"* I believe her input was sought because people viewed her contributions as significant, consistent, and selfless. She clearly articulated values she lived by, refusing to deviate from them. On the family front, she created for the eleven of us an environment where everyone felt safe, supported, and loved—where we were taught by example to be contributing members of wherever we found ourselves, personally and professionally.

Mother noted that under her high school graduation photo someone on the yearbook staff had written the words, *"None but her own could be her equal."* Truth be told, she valued excellence in every endeavor. Whether it was fulfilling her volunteer responsibilities or helping with homework, baking cookies for the Girl Scout bake sale, or creating from scratch the "King and Queen" chairs for the high school homecoming dance, tending to a sick child or neighbor, or typing monthly renewals for my father in his insurance business, she did everything with excellence. And she expected no less from the rest of us. She believed that if you did something, you should do it as though you were doing it for God. A tall order, indeed.

The words "good enough" were rarely used by my mother. She knew that the best and the brightest only got that way through personal effort and a commitment to developing their God-given gifts for the purpose of serving others. And whether it was her own child or one she had volunteered to teach to read or say prayers, she gave her time, effort, and full energy to the job. It could be said without a hint of hesitation that my mother's life consisted of giving her all, all the time, for the benefit of others.

My mother knew, long before the phrase "role modeling" found its way into our language, that *example* was the best teacher. She lived and demonstrated the values she believed in, with *love* and *family* at the top of her list and *care, compassion,* and *excellence* not far below. My mother had a servant leader's heart; she was a *contributor* and an enduring influence, not only to her children but also to others. Interactions with her almost always left people feeling better. My mother was a contributor of the highest order, and although she never held the title of leader, she led. In her community, volunteer organizations, church committees, and with her nine children, my mother led by serving as a quiet, consistent, and powerful role model.

Contribution: A Path to Enduring Influence

A leader's relationship with the people she services has a definite impact on the level of trust others have for the leader. If people know that the leader cares about what matters to them, and acts in ways that align with their interests, the leader's contribution to them increases their allegiance to her. Leaders who are an enduring influence are contributors. *Contribution* is the fourth cornerstone of leadership. The more you contribute to the needs of others, the higher the level of trust others give you. The more people who trust you, the greater your level of influence.

There may be times we begin wondering if we can successfully combine all that goes along with raising a family while seriously pursuing a career, or if it's possible to actually leave something of significance behind in both of these important arenas of our lives. Considering that the leaders in this book have demonstrated that, indeed, it can be done, I know beyond all doubt that it is possible for any of us, though we may have to pace ourselves, depending on what phase of life we are in. Do keep in mind that if you have a deep and genuine desire to serve others—to live life with the ever-present consciousness that the only way to experience meaningful success lies in being of service to others, then you are definitely a candidate for being an enduring influence and leaving your own lasting legacy. To explore a life of *contribution*, let's take a closer look at the three Ls of Contribution.

The Three *Ls* of Contribution:

Lead a life of service.
Leave a lasting legacy.
Look after what's been entrusted to you.

THE ENDURING INFLUENCE OF CONTRIBUTION

L eadership is synonymous with contribution—contribution of time, energy, resources, support, ideas, discoveries, and knowledge to those both inside and outside the organization. In this section you will see how our twelve leaders were exemplary service providers to their people, their peers, their profession, and their communities. You will get an inside look at how individual contributions so often result in leaving a lasting legacy, though there were no thoughts of such grandeur at the time. By instilling the practices of the four cornerstones of leadership, you have the potential of transforming the places and people you work with by your vision, decisions, and example. It all gets down to being a conscientious, courageous steward of all that has been entrusted to you.

CHAPTER 14

LEAD A LIFE OF SERVICE

*"Service is the rent that you pay for room
on this earth." –Shirley Chisholm*

My dear friend Lyla Fox died unexpectedly in the spring, just when it seemed that everything else was coming to life. She entered the hospital on a Tuesday and died three days later. The suddenness of her death was shocking, and for me it served as a poignant reminder of the importance of *now* and the futility of focusing on life's trivialities in all its many forms.

People showed up in droves from all over the country to attend her memorial and express their love for a woman who had first loved them. Lyla's memorial service, (originally expected to last an hour) had to be cut short after two and a half hours because so many people were intent on sharing their memories of this special woman. Friends didn't talk about her accomplishments as an author (although two of her Cozy Cat Mysteries had just been published, with a third on the way), nor did they speak about how she was loved as a school teacher or university instructor by scores of young men and women and their parents.

Instead, some people talked about Lyla and the impact she'd had on their lives, the big and small things she'd done to make life better for them: her handmade baby blankets (sometimes for total strangers), Raggedy Ann dolls she'd hand-crafted and given away, the sweaters, hats and scarves she'd knitted and given as gifts to babies and grand-babies of her friends. Others spoke of the beautiful Christmas tree skirts she'd made as gifts, the encouragement she offered to those who had lost hope, and the money she'd quietly handed over for medical bills, college tuition, or graduation gifts. There were stories by and about families she'd helped financially at holidays, letters of comfort and support she'd written, as well as the food she'd cooked and brought to a new mom, sick friend, or a grieving spouse.

Yet others told stories about the help she'd provided for those in need, providing access to services unknown to them, friends and relatives to whom she'd given her time, talent, heart and money to support in one way or the other. Lyla did all this and more, while working full time. She built competence and life-changing confidence in her students, championed causes that were important to her, and wrote articles for *Newsweek* and other national publications. She still was able to reserve her best for her children and husband. I can honestly say without hesitation that Lyla was one of the most curious, interesting, talented, giving, radiant people I have ever known—the likes of which will never pass this way again. Her memorial highlighted the fact that Lyla knew what was truly important in life. She chose to contribute rather than get bogged down with life's trivial, inconsequential matters.

When I think about the trap of the trivial, I'm reminded of the fable about a lion and a leopard: Both thirsty, the animals arrive at their usual watering hole at the same time. They immediately begin arguing about which of them should get to satisfy their thirst first. The argument becomes heated, and each decides he would rather die than sacrifice the privilege of being the first to drink. As they stubbornly confront each other, their emotions turn to rage and a fight ensues. Their cruel attacks on each other are suddenly interrupted. They both look up. Circling overhead flies a flock of vultures waiting for the loser to fall. Quietly, the two beasts turn and walk away. The thought of being devoured was all they needed to end their squabble.

Lyla knew that the most important things in life were not power, fame, or worldly possessions, though she recognized the value of each. But she focused on the importance of what a person does: how each of us use our time, talent, and treasure in service to others. This is what made Lyla a leader whose legacy will last forever, deeply impressed within the hearts of all those she touched during her lifetime.

Living a life of service does not mean that you drop everything else and devote yourself to others. Service is a *way* of life; a state of *being*—both intellectual and emotional. It is an awareness that your purpose is to take a position of servant leader, assisting others in ways that make life better; more fulfilling, purposeful, and meaningful. You encourage others, help them develop their skills, and you advocate for them when needed. Leaders who live a life of service do what they do with a genuine sense of love, compassion, and commitment.

Compassion Connects with Contribution

An acquaintance of mine grew up in India. I'll never forget a story she told me that happened when she was a young girl. Every morning as she walked to the bus stop for her ride to school, she would see a man whose job it was to keep the street clear of leaves and trash. She remembers being struck by the sincerity and devotion that this man applied to his job of street sweeping, simple and menial though it was. During this period in her life, a hurricane devastated her town. Trees were uprooted, poor people lost their homes, and many died. Things came to a standstill while the community recovered from the devastation.

On the day her schools reopened, my friend walked to the bus stop, amazed at the wreckage she could still see so many weeks after the hurricane. Standing at the bus stop, she saw the street sweeper and stopped to speak with him for a moment. She asked about his family, knowing that as one who earned a very low income, that he probably lived in the area that was hit hardest by the hurricane. *"Is your family safe?"* she asked him. With a very sad, hesitating tone, he said, *"I lost my mother to the hurricane. She was old and was working in the field when the hurricane came. She could not walk fast enough to get to a shelter, and she was swept away in the storm."*

My friend expressed her sympathy and offered financial help (which he refused) and told him if there was ever anything he needed, she would ask her family to help out. The street sweeper thanked her, and as my friend turned to walk toward the bus stop, she saw him wipe away his tears, pick up his broom stick, and return to his work, carefully sweeping away debris, cautiously pulling broken branches out of the way, consciously making the street much safer for the people who would be passing by.

This story brought home to me the fact that living a life of service is based on a state of mind; that any job we do, no matter how humble, can be done with care, compassion, and conscious effort. Some might call it professionalism. As Mother Teresa said, *"It is not how much we do, but how much love we put into that action."*

Every one of the unstoppable women presented in this book has operated out of a deep sense of compassion for, and commitment to, the community her business serves and in which she lives. Mary Ellen Sheets started out her business with a strong sense of contribution and service. At the end of her first year of business with her trucking operation, Two Men and a Truck, she had made a total profit of $1000. She sat down and wrote ten checks of $100 each for different local charities and gave away her entire profits for that year. What an auspicious beginning to a new venture!

Martha Mertz had a similar genesis as a leader. The entire concept of her organization, ATHENA International, which awards women leaders for great leadership, came about as a result of her asking the question: *"What can I do to contribute?"* She realized that what she could contribute in her role as a board member of the Lansing Regional Chamber of Commerce was diversity of thought and ideas. She realized that a lack of female representation on the chamber board meant that numerous organizations were unable to have a seat (and a voice) at the table. Martha's contribution was bringing more female voices onto the board, and thus began ATHENA International. She says, *"I love bringing people together to collaborate. When I'm part of a group and we are truly there to join forces, everyone is valued, everyone is listened to, and everyone is heard. I think that's how you bring out the best in people, when they know that their presence is valued."* Martha's statement is indicative of her desire to value and encourage those who make worthy contributions to individuals in their service to the organization of which they are a part.

Contribution Implies Giving

Kathie VanderPloeg's parents instilled in her the importance of contribution. She says, *"Giving was ingrained in me as a child. My parents felt that our local community and our marketplace was so supportive of our business that we needed to give back. We learned how to do that from a very early age. In our business, part of our profit is set aside every year to contribute money to organizations we believe we need to be helping. We give to the community, and we give to the marketplace in the areas that we are serving."*

Servant leaders constantly seek opportunities to serve and give, and whether it is in the form of financial help, or personal encouragement and support, giving is key. Contribution flows from an inner desire to give—a listening ear, a kind word, helpful advice, time, money, energy, or expertise—whatever is needed by the individual or by the community.

Eleanor Roosevelt's entire life seemed powered by a devotion to contribution. She suffered from a painful lack of self-esteem due to her "plain looks" (which her mother ridiculed) and her perceived ineptness in the role that most women of her era were expected to play. She stepped out of the feminine stereotype to become a civil rights activist, a human rights champion, and a political diplomat. Eleanor Roosevelt's life was devoted to improving the lives of children, women, veterans, and minority workers, as well as the lives of countless others. She built no empires and led no nations, and though she died over 50 years ago, her legacy lives on through every generation since.

Lillian Bauder sums it up well when she says, *"Sometimes people think if you can be ambitious on your way up and aspire to be a great success, it doesn't matter what else happens because you're being upwardly mobile. In my life experience, at least, that has not been the case at all. Help others succeed. Enjoy what you do, and do what you enjoy, understand that kindness and generosity are never forgotten. There may be things that you forget, but people never do."*

When you live life with a mindset of giving and serving others, your opportunity to make a difference for your community is great. Contribution through service to others is consistently a characteristic of our greatest, most inspiring, and most memorable leaders.

CHAPTER 15

LEAVE A LASTING LEGACY

*"Leadership is about making others better as a
result of your presence and making sure that impact
lasts in your absence." –Sheryl Sandberg*

Mentoring Means Legacy: A Gift that Keeps on Giving

When I asked La June Tabron what accomplishments she was most proud of in her career, one of the first things she mentioned was her sense of pride in the number of people she has helped to empower. She said, *"I think of people in this organization who wanted to grow and develop, and I now stand back and look at them and think about how I was able to contribute to their growth and help them be what they wanted to be in this organization."* Her contribution to those she's mentored or helped in some way has not only served them but has expanded their reach, making it possible for them to touch even more lives and be of even greater value to the organization. Mentoring and empowering others allows La June and others like her to pass along their knowledge and wisdom and belief in the individual, just one way to leave a lasting legacy through the lives of other people.

Kathie VanderPloeg has extended her reach internationally. She mentors small business owners in Kenya as part of her involvement with a non-profit that provides micro-loan financing to entrepreneurs. She frequently travels back and forth to Kenya, taking time out of her busy schedule to contribute her experience to those who truly need it.

Lillian Bauder mentors others by sharing her vast experience gained in a variety of fields. She says, *"That is one of the side benefits of being a role model—people come to you, they can learn from you, you can help them individually, and it is wonderful to see when they succeed.* This is how the leader's legacy lives on.

Gail McGovern's decision to accept a leadership position at the American Red Cross came about as a result of her deep desire to continue the mentoring experience she began as a young girl working with inner city children. She realized that her corporate career had not provided her enough opportunities to contribute to the growth and development of others, and that accepting the offer to head up the Red Cross would be a wonderful way to do the "soul" work that she really needed to do.

Beth Jones regularly mentors and coaches young people who want to be pastors and church leaders in order to, as she says, *"Help others avoid some of those mistakes that we made so they can go further and faster than we did."*

Naomi Rhode puts mentoring those who will follow her at the top of her list for guaranteeing the ongoing success of the organization. She says, *"When I see such great qualities in younger people, younger in position, if not in age, I want to pull them through all of the hoops so that I can assure this association or this corporation will have great leadership when I step down."*

All of our unstoppable women leaders have demonstrated that it is not enough to just lead and be successful as an individual. True leadership is about producing more leaders, not more followers. When a leader succeeds in creating or developing other unstoppable leaders, she has left a legacy for future generations.

Passing on wisdom and knowledge, as we have seen throughout this book, takes many forms. For instance, when our twelve leaders agreed to be interviewed for this book, they committed to helping you and other readers learn from their own experiences, possibly contributing to your future success. The information they provided can serve as inspiration for you by the ways they guided, suggested, and encouraged potential in their employees. You can use their wisdom and practices as a model for developing your potential and providing your employees with opportunities to grow. By giving of themselves and passing along their experiences, these outstanding women contribute to the careers of others in ways that ensures a leader's legacy. It warms my heart to know that you will do the same.

Legacies Live On

While scouring the Internet, I discovered the amazing story of Joe E. Martin, a police officer and boxing coach who mentored and coached two of the world's greatest boxing champions. In 1954, a 12-year old African American boy from a poor family came up to Martin, complaining that a thief stole his bike. The angry child said he was going to "whup" the thief. The meeting with Martin changed this young man's life forever. Instead of merely writing down the lad's complaint and helping to locate his bike, Martin told the young man that he would help him "whup" the thief, provided he learn how to box. For a few years, Martin took this kid under his wing, coaching and encouraging him. Six years later, that same young man went on to win Olympic gold. Martin's mentee, the victorious Olympic boxing champion, was none other than Muhammad Ali.[19]

In 1977 Martin was inducted into the Amateur Boxing Hall of Fame as one of the world's greatest coaches. Did Martin know at the time he met the young kid whose bike got stolen that he would go on to become one of the greatest, most famous heavyweight boxing champions in the world? I highly doubt it.

All he knew was that he had an opportunity to redirect the life of one child from a disadvantaged background with limited resources to one where he could learn boxing, an empowering skill that might build his confidence and self-regard. In the process, Martin discovered an amazing talent in this young man to whom he gave a life of meaning and purpose. He developed a champion boxer who has also mentored and coached hundreds of other young people from various walks of life to find their purpose. In mentoring Muhammad Ali, Martin created a lasting legacy of mentorship that will live for many generations.

Great leaders know that what makes leaving a legacy so meaningful is that it can take on a "life of its own" through others in perpetuity, whether through family members, employees, the effects of organizational transformation, the founding of an award, or social or political change as the result of a cause. In other words, each leader touches the life of one person or perhaps several, and these individuals in turn mentor, teach, or in some way touch the life of another. And the cycle repeats itself over and over.

Naomi Rhode puts it succinctly when she says, *"We are given a* plethora of platforms. It could be the platform of marriage or the platform of teaching a child integrity-based concepts, or system improvements in our workplace. If we see the process as an amazing privilege, one we can instill in someone else—leaving our legacy can be very powerful."

CHAPTER 16

LOOK AFTER WHAT'S ENTRUSTED TO YOU

"Be faithful in small things because it is in them your strength lies." –Mother Theresa

L eaders who achieve uncommon success are the people who step into leadership out of a desire to serve a greater good; they do not seek leadership roles for the purpose of being in charge, but for the purpose of being of service. As any good servant leader, they operate as responsible stewards of all that has been entrusted to their care, including an organization's people and its mission and vision. They see a larger purpose for the work they do, and they see themselves playing a vital role in changing the way the organization operates, making it more productive and more valuable. They help create greater levels of satisfaction for themselves and those who work for their growing, changing, evolving organization.

You may be familiar with the *Parable of the Talents* in which a master gives each of three servants a number of talents according to their individual abilities, and eventually calls them to give account for how they had increased the value of what they had been given.[20] Leaders, too, eventually are called upon to account for what has been entrusted to them. And the expectation is that the organization each servant leader is responsible for will flourish in her care.

The Privilege of Entrustment

When Naomi Rhode became the president of the National Speakers Association, her chosen theme for that year was *The Privilege of the Platform.*

Naomi clearly understood that professional speaking was a platform that carries a great deal of responsibility and accountability for each person who takes the stage. She felt strongly that professional speaking should be considered a calling, that speakers are not on the platform to elevate their position or stroke their ego, but to serve: to expand perspectives, enhance knowledge, and share wisdom. Naomi felt passionately about the speaker's enormous responsibilities to the organizations and the audiences they serve, and that's why she chose the word *privilege*. A humble leader, Naomi understands stewardship, and she knows that good stewardship is *payment* for the privilege of being given the awesome opportunity of addressing an audience. She did not want the speaking platform to be something her members took lightly. She felt the same way about assuming leadership roles in the association; that it was an honor and privilege, and it was every leader's responsibility to be good stewards of the trust they had been given by association members.

Naomi Rhode understood that stewardship goes beyond responsibility. It holds an expectation that leaders will take good care of that which has been entrusted to them. At the heart of good stewardship resides a desire to serve, a desire to care for all involved, a belief in the greater purpose and vision in which people see themselves playing an instrumental role. I feel compelled to add that success in any lofty venture begins and ends with diligent caring for ourselves, our health, personal development, and our families. Without care for self, it is almost impossible to sustain the energy to care for someone or something else in the grand scheme of things.

Looking After Yourself: Personal Stewardship

The women I interviewed for this book spoke about, or implied, the importance of "work-life balance" as being critical to their success as a leader. They all talked about the support provided by their loved ones, spouses, children, and friends. Gail McGovern says that her biggest supporters are her husband and her brother, attributing much of her effectiveness to their advice.

Cheryle Touchton similarly depends upon the support of her family— her husband, her children, her grandchildren, and her elderly parents—and works hard to be one hundred percent present to her family when spending time with them and one hundred percent present to her work when working. But that wasn't always the case. Early in her career, when she was with her children, she felt guilty about not doing more at work, and, when at work, she felt guilty about not being with her children. She says, *"I wish I had understood sooner that wherever I am is where I am supposed to be, and that I am to give my best there."* Today, she carves out a niche to be with her family and spends time with each one of them, taking time away from work. Other times, work demands take time away from her family. But to this she says, *"Instead of torturing myself about it, I just accept the reality of the situation and handle the work things I need to handle and the family things I need to handle. I give them each my best, and I walk away feeling like what I did was enough."*

Mary Ellen Sheets' support comes from her husband and her three children who currently play vital roles in her organization. At a time when she was exhausted by her work, her children stepped up to take on some of her major responsibilities.

Ruth Shaw prioritized her life in such a way that her career and her family were her main focus areas. This did not leave time for much else. She feels satisfied with the choices she made because she said that, had she tried to do it all, she would have taken time from her four most important priorities: her husband, her two sons, and her mother. Her joy today comes from the friendships she's formed and the support she receives from others who serve on the same boards as she.

Mary Ellen Rodgers has always been aware of the importance of work-life balance. She talks about the importance of having a personal North Star—that which has allowed her to recognize *what's* important *when* and to make decisions accordingly. Whenever faced with a situation where two priorities clash (work and family, for example), Mary Ellen advises us to compare the criticality of the event with the role. For example, there are times when, in her role as a mother, watching her son participate in a football game is more important than any work activity. So, she will prioritize that sporting event over work.

At another time, a work priority critical to her role as managing partner at Deloitte may come first. For Mary Ellen, her personal North Star helps her to figure that out. It is a constant balancing act and not a cake walk. But this is the only way that a leader can ensure that she gives equal

LOOK AFTER WHAT'S ENTRUSTED TO YOU

attention and care to her family as well as to her work. She says, *"That personal North Star helps you avoid wasting a lot of energy on whether to say yes or no; it helps you not to be conflicted in terms of work and personal decisions—and this is very freeing. At least it is for me."*

Lillian Bauder found out the hard way that without work-life balance, she could not really succeed in her personal life, nor have time to develop fully. Lillian talks about her days at Cranbrook Educational Community when she gradually and inadvertently relegated her home and family life to the background in order to concentrate on issues at Cranbrook that she describes as *"pervasive year around"* and never ending. After 14 years (and 44 weeks of lost vacations), her husband had created an independent life of his own in her absence. The two evening meals a week with him that her demanding schedule allowed were truly inadequate. Realizing what she had put at risk, she decided to make some changes. Lillian and her husband rekindled their relationship and discovered each other anew. She also rekindled her personal interest in poetry and began engaging in other activities that interested her.

Lillian fully admits that the struggle between work and one's personal life is a balancing act, and a price you have to pay. She says, *"It is a ceaseless effort that is never completely successful; it is never-ending and has elements of success and elements of failure within it continuously. Still, a full life is worth that. I have led an extraordinarily full life and feel very blessed to have had that."*

Naomi Rhode advises people who don't have the support of their families to form a substitute family of friends that can provide you with the kind of support you would normally expect from your family. She says, *"I would suggest that if someone doesn't have a ready-made support system that they create one by making a family out of people who are mutually supportive. Everybody needs to be supported and encouraged at times. Encouragement from family helps to put things in a better balance. Adopt some sisters and brothers and choose them carefully. Build those relationships into trusting, caring, and mutually beneficial opportunities."*

Caring for our health is another aspect of good stewardship. You cannot hope to sustain the hectic life of a proactive leader without investing in your health. Mary Ellen Rodgers talks about the importance of vacations as a means to regenerate your creativity. When she started her career in the early 1980s, she was told by one of her partners that in order to be successful, she would have to come in to work an hour early and be the last one to leave at night. As Mary Ellen grew professionally, she realized that it was some of the worst advice she had ever received. Without taking breaks to relax and de-stress, leaders simply cannot perform at their best. She now advises women to take breaks whenever they can in order to step back and restore their sense of balance. That includes activities like walking or yoga at lunch breaks, spending time with the family, or taking vacations. She says, *"As leaders, we owe it to younger people to tell them that the work is tough, and it is our personal responsibility to figure out how we can get energy from our work and take personal time to bring our best to the workplace on a consistent basis."*

Caring for Your Team is Stewardship, Too

Good stewardship is also about caring for the health and work-life balance of your team. From knowing names and circumstances, to asking about the health of family members, to helping out financially when needed, or simply listening, each leader has worked hard to allow her people to serve to the best of their abilities by providing encouragement, mentoring, education, and emotional support.

For example, Gail McGovern creates a caring environment for her team members by encouraging them to bring a bit of their family life to work, such as photographs or memorabilia. She says, *"When I think of my direct reporting team, I know every one of their spouses' names; I know every one of their kids' names; I know when one of their children has a big soccer playoff. If they come in and say, 'I have to leave; there is a school play,' I kick them out."* McGovern knows that when you care for your people, they will care for you and the organization.

Despite being retired, Mary Ellen Sheets continues to care for her employees. While she managed the business, she managed to make it a point to hold family picnics and get-togethers for her team members so that she could get to know them personally. She continues the tradition. She says, *"When people have babies, I will buy a bunch of baby things and bring them in to show that I care about their families. We have office picnics where employees bring their kids, or dogs, and I get to know them all. It's important to personally show you care for people around you. Always put others first. If it is your customers or your employees, try to think and do everything the best way you can for them, so you'll have good outcomes."*

Patricia Caruso cared not just for her employees, but also for the prisoners for whom she was responsible as warden and later as director of the Michigan Department of Corrections. She says that on visits to prisons when she was the director, prisoners would come up to her and thank her for the way she cared for them in her role as warden. They remembered her kindness and her compassion. This genuine caring underlined her efforts to reform prisons and rehabilitate prisoners by training and educating them to live as responsible members of society rather than be incarcerated for life without being given a second chance.

Good stewardship permeates every area of a leader's responsibility. A good steward recognizes that the care she gives to everything with which she has been entrusted—developing herself and her people, building a shared vision for the organization, maintaining her commitment to the truth, and making the best decisions regarding policies, strategies, and systems—all work to shape the organization and the direction it takes. These are all a part of the duty and responsibility of the leader who is unstoppable, able to succeed at the highest level. Because a good leader, like a good parent, makes a commitment to the growth and transformation of the organization and the people in it, she recognizes, and accepts the enormity of the role she undertakes.

Leaders Make a Lasting Contribution

Great leadership is synonymous with contribution. A leader's contributions are numerous and varied, from the personal to the professional, the intellectual to the emotional, the theoretical to the practical. The road is not an easy one. But, if at the heart of the leader there exists a genuine desire to serve, she cannot help but to expand her territory in terms of knowledge, wisdom, and discernment, while, at the same time, care deeply for the people she serves. When the servant leader does these things, she stands a good chance of being counted among those leaders who reach the top—someone other people will seek to emulate. Her legacy will live on within those who follow in her footsteps.

CHAPTER 17

CONCLUSION

THE LEADER NEXT DOOR

"Be who you were created to be, and you will set the world on fire." –Catherine of Siena

We've established that the most successful women leaders have vision, fortitude, and the ability to work in competitive environments without compromising their values, unique traits, and skill sets. They work with a level of internal alignment that naturally generates respect and collaboration. They are women who believe in themselves and their ability to learn, even from mistakes, and they believe in, value, and seek out what others can bring to the table.

They are women who nurture relationships and vital connections inside and outside of their organizations. They work cooperatively and collaboratively with others to accomplish goals that advance the vision and mission of their organizations. They are not only aligned with their own values, but they also strongly identify with, and support, the values of their organizations.

According to *The Mysterious Success of Female-Led Firms*, an article written by Stephanie Marton: *Women business leaders have differentiated themselves as strong decision-makers. Research suggests that women at the helm of companies and investment portfolios tend to outperform their male counterparts, domestically and internationally.*[21] Though the reasons are not definitive, this demonstrates that women leaders, who tend to operate differently from the traditional male model (mentioned throughout this book), bring high levels of value to their organizations, communities, and families.

Leaders Make a Difference

It is my fervent hope that our twelve unstoppable leaders have inspired you with their wisdom, buoyancy, and fortitude. I hope you feel a sense of excitement about your own potential by deciding to remain committed to self-development. I hope you will be so inspired you'll continue cultivating the leadership skills and traits indicative of those who leave an enduring leadership legacy.

I intentionally chose the twelve extraordinary leaders to feature in this book because none of them are famous, yet each of them have made, or are making, a difference at the highest levels. I included examples and stories about other women who have made a difference to make the point that women of high caliber are everywhere. Look around. You don't have to look far to find other powerful, effective women operating at exceptional levels who have their own stories about their journeys to the top of their fields. Many of these women are a lot like you; they have the drive and desire to make a difference.

Leaders: They're Everywhere

In my mind the "leader next door" is an ordinary woman who is accomplishing extraordinary results. She is leading others to believe in her vision to the point that they willing pledge their loyalty and energy to fulfill it. She has developed the required character by remaining personally aligned, withstanding adversity, and making the right choices for her team and organization or cause.

She has the commitment to pursue her passion regardless of the odds, and she is able to communicate her vision to the team. She studies and practices the principles that drive the heart and mind of a true leader (character, commitment, core work, and contribution). The work of a leader is to cultivate possibility. She possesses the scope to connect present situations with positive potential outcomes, whether it involves a person or a project. She has the ability to garner the resources to fulfill her vision (despite the challenges), enabling her to leave a lasting legacy. And the best part? Not only is her environment (or cause) all the better for her contributions, she too is enriched by the experience.

Everyone has Leadership Potential

Women who possess many of the traits of our twelve unstoppable lead ers come from everywhere and from all kinds of backgrounds, and I encourage you to look for them in your own back yard for inspiration and perhaps collaboration. In reading the stories and examples in this book, stay keenly tuned to what's possible for you, right where you are. You may or may not aspire to be the CEO of a major corporation, educational institution, non-profit agency, or association. You may or may not wish to become the founder and president of your own small business or take the reins of an existing business or start up.

Yet you may be yearning to contribute in unique ways, to have an influence, to make a difference in your workplace or community, your place of worship, within your family, or a cause that is special to you. And you can. Like everyday citizens such as Candy Lightner and others like her who have embraced a vision or cause and taken the lead, so can you, provided you are willing to do what's required.

You may have noticed that many of the twelve leaders featured in this book hail from Michigan, my home state. Several of them have lived or worked within 100 miles of where I live; some still do. This brings home the point that there are exceptional women everywhere, doing extraordinary things; that there truly are all kinds of leaders in our own back yards.

In this chapter I hope you enjoy the reports of ordinary women exercising extraordinary leadership at a local level; women who are following their passion, cultivating relationships, making a difference, and leaving a legacy.

Colleen Munson: Leadership is More Than a Game

Meet Colleen Munson, head volleyball coach at Western Michigan University. Seriously committed to the twelve girls on her volleyball team, Colleen approaches her job as head coach in a unique way. She sees her job, first and foremost, as the keeper of the mission she and her staff have set for themselves: *To empower and equip confident student athletes to become impactful leaders, teammates, and winners as life-long members of the WMU volleyball team.*

Colleen starts recruiting early, always on the lookout for players with the skill sets she needs to replace. But more than that, she looks for young women who possess specific character traits as well. This double focus, on not just physical skill but mental outlook, sets her program apart from others. When student athletes arrive on campus with their families to research the WMU volleyball team, they are presented with a rigorous assessment to determine who will be the best fit for the team.

Colleen and her staff don't just focus on technique or game strategy; potential players are presented with a series of character-based questions as well. As uncomfortable as it might be for the visiting athletes, answering questions that define character and ethics gives Colleen and her staff a fuller picture of each player and how she would or would not be a good fit for the team.

Once the season begins in August, Colleen meets with her players once a week to read and discuss books supporting the values and standards of accountability, discipline and pride. Discussions involve who they are as people, the belief being if they can become confident athletes, volleyball success will follow. From August to December, the girls grow exponentially, learning to serve one another as teammates, which in turn serves their personal development.

Colleen reminds her players and staff, *"If anything goes against our values, then we don't want to be doing it."* This helps her young women develop leadership qualities so they can learn to thrive in their world of WMU volleyball and grow as individuals and leaders. Of course, this doesn't happen overnight, but by junior year, players faithfully serve their team, having discovered that by serving the whole, not only are there team benefits, but personal ones as well.

Beating the Odds

In August 2014, they had the makings of a championship team. But then, things fell apart. Within ten days, one team leader became pregnant and had to be replaced. The brother of another player was reported missing and later was found dead. After a player's grandfather died, she went home to be with her family for nearly two weeks.

Over the next few months, team members experienced ankle sprains, a back injury, and two concussions, with each player out for a month. The staff wasn't doing much better. Add the passing of a grandparent, followed by a miscarriage for the wife of a staff member, and the death of yet another grandfather.

As you can imagine, with so much happening, Colleen's team had less than a stellar season. Yet, everyone held onto their big vision and persevered, thanks to Colleen's mentoring, leading, and supporting. Despite the setbacks and losses, at season's end they had qualified for the Mid-America Conference, from which the winning team would receive an automatic bid to the NCAA tournament, their ultimate goal.

As the Mid-America Conference rolled around, the WMU team had suffered so many setbacks that no one expected them to win, including the athletic director who told Colleen to *"just go have fun."* But Colleen, her staff, and the players knew their vision was bigger than that.

As the team stepped on the bus and took off for the tournament in Athens, OH, they left the naysayers and bad vibes behind. Scheduled to play an unheard of four matches in three days, the players focused on their vision and what they had practiced, repeatedly, over the previous four months. It didn't matter that no one expected them to win. That wasn't their focus.

Going into the semi-finals, they were 0 – 2 (Volleyball matches are the best 3 out of 5 so their prospects didn't look good). Clearly, they were the underdogs. But the players remained focused, confident, and totally engaged. They had been mentored and developed into competent, outstanding players and leaders who knew how to serve their team.

Under Colleen's leadership, her team of twelve had come to understand the importance of developing strong character, adhering to uncompromised commitment, doing their core work, and contributing to the good of the whole. Although they were down by two games, and against all odds, they persevered. The team went to five sets against the best team in their conference—and went home with the trophy. They had won the Mid-America Conference Tournament.

Whether work or sports team, corporation or small business, community or faith-based group, or even an individual mission, there is no substitute for unflinching character, unstoppable commitment, and deeply embedded core work for making a contribution that results in long-lasting benefits for all. Do leaders make a difference? Colleen Munson is one prime example.

Cindi Alwood: Following a Dream

Some leaders make a mark so deep and wide their names become a household word. Others consistently and quietly follow their dream. The latter describes Cindie Alwood, Director of the Women's Center of Greater Lansing, located in Michigan's capital city.

Self-described as a *"social activist and the only kid in my family to graduate from college,"* with a Bachelor of Arts degree in Speech Pathology and Audiology from Western Michigan University and a Master's degree in Rehabilitation Counseling from Michigan State University, Cindie always had a spot in her heart for the struggles of disabled and disadvantaged women, particularly victims of violence.

While serving as a national hotline volunteer for a political action group, Cindie answered calls from women facing various critical issues. Some were involved in, or had just escaped, violent relationships or had faced sexual harassment in the workplace. Many were middle-aged, uninsured, and in need of medical attention or public services. Sadly, there was no local resource that could provide assistance beyond offering shelter for abused women.

Building the Dream

After she and a like-minded friend researched this distressing service gap in depth, they decided to create a place where women with no money, no insurance, and limited resources could reinvent their lives. From the beginning, there were hurdles. Only with intervention from Michigan Senator Debbie Stabenow did they receive 501c3 (nonprofit) status. It took time to find an affordable space close to downtown, located on a major bus line to accommodate women without cars.

Cindie and her colleague purchased two buildings side by side, both in a state of massive disrepair, but affordable. Both co-directors contacted everyone they knew, asking for help in demolition and construction. The first workday, it was a frigid zero degrees, yet twenty-seven people showed up to help. For a solid month, a skilled, all-female volunteer crew, plus a lone male plumber, showed up and did the work. Those less handy with tools supplied home-cooked meals for the workers. The first board meeting took place in January 2005 in an unheated room with everyone bundled in coats and hats, sharing their dreams of what the center would become. On June 21, 2005 the Women's Center of Greater Lansing opened its doors. From then to now, the women served are in need of employment due to divorce or abandonment, death of a spouse, organizational downsizing, or failed businesses. The employment goal for each client is to find one good-paying position instead of two or three jobs with no benefits.

Part of Cindie's dream was accessibility. Fees are on a sliding schedule based on ability to pay, starting at $1.00. The center accepts no insurance. When the economic downturn hit, the number of clients skyrocketed; women who had lost their jobs or homes were calling, desperate for help. No one was turned away nor charged a fee.

Before Cindie and her volunteer team can expect clients to find and hold onto a job, there are mental health issues to consider, especially when trauma from violence exists. Counselors first assess a client's state of mind and stability level before they pursue finding suitable employment.

Instilling the Dream

In the center's program called, "Work Your Image," clients receive an external makeover to complement the internal support, offering tips on grooming, social and self-presentation skills. They learn what constitutes suitable attire for interviews, and they find such outfits in the center's collection of donated interview-appropriate clothing.

Dental health is a big factor in making a good impression. Early on, Cindie cemented relationships with local dentists willing to provide gratis services for women who would otherwise suffer chronic pain or embarrassment because of their appearance. Cindie described one such client. *"A woman came in some months ago with her infant. Living in a domestic violence shelter, she was so sick she could barely care for the baby. Poor nutrition had taken its toll; her teeth were literally falling out. She avoided eye contact and refused to smile, she was so embarrassed about her mouth. We found a local dentist who donated several thousand dollars' worth of work.*

This woman, smart and determined, is still a work in progress, yet has come so far. She smiles now, will look you in the eye, and shake your hand. She's working on her Associate's degree and her dream is to become an accountant." Cindie has hundreds of stories about women who cultivated the personal and professional skills needed to achieve financial self-sufficiency.

In 2008 the Women's Center of Greater Lansing became one of the premier agencies for counseling and social work interns hailing from several of Michigan's major universities to serve the center's clients. Though the center does receive some grants, it relies mostly on personal donations, a monthly donor program, and annual fund-raising events, one of which is aptly called "Dream, Girl!" The buildings are paid for, grant monies and donations trickle in to sustain operations, and volunteers help with building maintenance, landscaping, and assorted repairs.

The ongoing Job Group offers classes covering resume and cover letter writing, interviewing skills, and other practicalities of job search. The computer lab offers classes and skill training on the latest technologies to keep clients current. Women have many options, depending on their needs, from counseling or personal growth classes, to finishing a degree or finding employment. A few have even launched their own businesses.

Despite its long list of testimonials from women served, this is not a Cinderella story of a small local resource that made it big. Due to the nature of its clients and services, the center often doesn't meet the rigid criteria of major grants. But thanks to faithful donors and small to midsized grants, the center continues doing what it does best, helping women redirect the course of their lives.

Cindie's dream, providing pathways for women facing hard times or escaping the cycle of violence, has become a reality. She made the commitment, formed relationships, and forged ahead with fortitude even when things looked bleak. The Women's Center of Greater Lansing has so far brought hope, help, and healing to over 6,000 women. Cindie Alwood, leading her mostly volunteer team and one staff member, has passionately and persistently held onto her dream of helping women reinvent themselves and enrich their lives, and as a result, enrich their local community as well.

Erin Oakley: Leadership for the Love of It

Meet Erin Oakley, a full-time homemaker and mother of two, who found her way into a book on leadership because of the contributions she had made out of love. This humble sports enthusiast has made quite a name for herself, not out of ambition but of service. Erin loves to play disc golf (also known as Frisbee golf), and through her passion and persistence, Erin single-handedly changed the nature of the game for women in her home state of Michigan. Traditionally a male-dominated sport, Erin wanted to see more women involved in her sport.

Thanks to her vision and irresistible influence, Michigan is the home of an annual two-day women's disc golf tournament (Disc Girls Gone Wild), founded nearly a decade ago. Aside from Women's Nationals, this competitive event has become one of the *premiere* women-only tournaments in the world, drawing players from novice level to pro from numerous states throughout the US and a few foreign countries as well. Just the planning for such an event (choosing the courses, inviting and registering players, securing sponsorships, organizing food and lodging, soliciting volunteers, finding officials, and prizes) would be enough to deter a weaker soul. But Erin thrives on these organizational duties and competes in the tournament as well.

A player for sixteen years now, Erin clung to her desire to start a disc golf league for local women, with the intent of having fun rather than focusing on competition. Her first effort failed, but she tried again in 2005 and this time she succeeded. Every year the membership continues to grow. A professional level player, Erin invites and recruits women at all skill levels and ages (ranging from nine years old to the mid-seventies). She lovingly mentors and coaches new players, and offers she clinics to league members for finessing their skills and learning game rules and etiquette. She presents free demonstrations at parks, encourages school administrators to add disc golf to their sports curriculum, and tirelessly volunteers at outdoor events to raise awareness about the game she loves so much. When it comes to promoting disc golf, Erin is unstoppable.

In the past, only a handful of women showed up for Michigan's statewide disc golf championships compared with a lengthy roster of male players because the only divisions that existed for women were at the pro and advanced levels. Erin persuaded the state organization to offer divisions at the lower (amateur) levels, and, not surprisingly, record numbers of women now compete in the annual championships, many of them from Erin's local league.

The Feat Goes On

As a long-time member of the Professional Disc Golf Association, Erin has served for four years on the PDGA Women's Committee, the purpose of which is to get women more involved in the game locally and globally. It's working. In the last decade there's been an appreciable increase in the number of women players belonging to PDGA, more women's leagues popping up around the world, and more women-only tournaments across North America. So far, two biannual Global Women's Events have been held, involving players from countries around the world who compete in their respective divisions, on their local courses, all on the same day. Records are kept and prizes are given. As a PDGA Women's Committee member, Erin was involved in conceiving and coordinating this ever-growing event.

When she can swing it, Erin competes at a national level and has become well known in the disc golf community for her friendliness, humility, and strength of character. In 2012 the PDGA presented her with the Bob West Memorial Sportsmanship Award. And thanks to Erin's example and enthusiasm there are now three thriving women's leagues in her state, a silent testimony to her dream of putting women's disc golf on the Michigan map.

In each of our communities, there exist a surprising number of women making contributions with purpose and passion, that idea of the *leader next door*, and Erin Oakley is a fine example of the difference one fully committed person can make. It's not for money or fame, but just for the love of it. This unassuming woman with a supportive husband and two daughters, who will probably one day follow in their mother's footsteps, is a force to be reckoned with in the most positive context possible.

Erin, with her giving heart and buoyant spirit, has added value to the lives of untold sports-minded girls and women within her state and far beyond, simply because she loves the game and wants others to love it, too. Erin is convinced that there's much more she can do for women who play disc golf. If all the changes she's supported, initiated, and improved upon so far are not an example of making a difference, I don't know what is.

Amy Geil Susan: If You Build it, They Will Come

Amy Geil Susan is a nineteen-year veteran Account Executive at Promotion Concepts, Inc., located in Kalamazoo, Michigan. She holds a Bachelor of

Business Administration degree from Western Michigan University and is married to Justin, her college sweetheart, and "mother" to her two-year-old Daisy Dog, Murphy. Upon meeting her, Amy Susan would probably strike you as the friendly, likeable woman you'd be apt to meet at a backyard neighborhood barbeque. But spend any time with her, and she'd knock your socks off with her extraordinary ability to sell her vision, win people over, and lead them in support of her many charitable causes.

For the first 10 years of her marriage, Amy Susan organized fun events for the women in the community. They called themselves the *Cloud 9 Chicks*. This 100 percent totally social group grew to over 300 participants. She said, *"I knew that God had planted all of these wonderful women in my life for a reason, and that one day I could use these solid relationships for something special."*

It began with the "Oh Baby!" event she created for the March of Dimes, where she invited attendees to fill a child's play pen to the rim with donated goods for the local Bronson Children's Hospital. Then there was her "Brighton & Bravo" event at the local Moors Golf Club where she gathered her ever-expanding social group to see the new fall collection of Brighton® Jewelry, and, at the same time, contribute new or gently used bras for the local YWCA. Her events are always a huge hit and a boat-load of fun. Visualize bras brandishing chandeliers in the country club, or dangling from the antlers of a wall-mounted moose head, and you can imagine gales of sidesplitting laughter. While Amy admits that life can be pretty serious, as a community leader, she is wedded to infusing a bit of silliness and a whole lot of *fun* in everything she does.

I first met Amy when she was organizing Habi Hour, an auction in support of one of her favorite non-profits, Habitat for Humanity. Amy first became interested in Habitat after witnessing a home blessing dedication ceremony for a new Habitat homeowner. She was deeply moved, believing that every human being should have a healthy, affordable place to call home.

From Small Venue to a Big Vision

Habi Hour began as a simple gathering of friends at Amy's home. A friend from her church offered to play music, a neighbor offered to brew four styles of craft beer, and, all of the sudden, she had a group of more than seventy friends who were more than willing to support this worthy cause. She held a small silent auction offering an eclectic assortment of items in her garage where paint cans were used for décor. She sprinkled colored glitter all over the floor for effect and loves that much of it still sparkles on the surface yet today. From this small gathering the seeds for future commitment were planted by friends whom Amy persuaded to follow her in support of the non-profit.

After the success of that first Habi Hour auction, Amy, whose favorite line from the movie *Field of Dreams* is *"If you build it, they will come,"* believed this concept could play out on a much grander scale. During this period, one of Kalamazoo's best-loved breweries, Bell's Brewery (and a very important client to her company), was adding a state-of-the-art entertainment venue to their existing structure. Amy knew that if she, with the help of friends and the Brewery's staff, "built" a signature charity event for Kalamazoo Valley Habitat for Humanity that *"they would come."* With the promise of great music, great friends, great Michigan craft beer, and a great event location, come they did! For four years Habi Hour has boasted a sold out crowd annually, raising over $125,000 for Kalamazoo Valley Habitat for Humanity.

Amy attributes her success to great relationships, her ability to keep volunteers happy and committed, to her staying focused, organized, and keeping the end goal in mind. She believes that an infusion of positive energy and *fun* keeps people motivated and interested in being active participants in a cause, making them willing to do the hard work necessary for success.

From my experience volunteering on a Habi project with Amy at the helm, I know firsthand that she brings far more than focus, organization, and fun. Amy Susan is a leader driven by a passion for making a difference and has the ability to communicate her vision. She knows the difference she can help make in the lives of others. Her genuine love for people and the potential each holds is consistently demonstrated through an uncanny ability to get everyone working in unity, cooperating, and collaborating every step of the way, regardless of the size of the group.

She is quick to show appreciation for the gifts others bring to the table, always open to hearing new and creative ideas. Regardless of whether those ideas are used or not, each person ends up feeling good about their contribution because all ideas are heard and discussed and decided upon in a fair fashion.

Amy Susan admits that though she and the "crew" she assembles never really know how an endeavor will turn out, she walks by faith, spending time in prayer, asking for guidance every step of the way. She readily admits that the two most influential books in her life regarding how to relate to and treat other people have been *The Bible* and Dale Carnegie's *How to Win Friends and Influence People*, a book she was given at age ten by Donna Sweet, the woman Amy calls, "Granny Gran Crackers."

Amy says that serving others is her greatest joy, and her actions throughout her entire adult life certainly prove it. She is captivated by the thought of the enormous difference one person can make in the lives of others. Recently elected as a board member to the Animal Rescue Project, Amy cheerfully quips, *"I can't wait to see what God has in store for me with this new endeavor."*

Neither can I after having seen this "leader next door" in action, creating vision, crafting teams, and leading a life of service. If past performance is any indication, a great deal of success is in store for the organizations in which Amy Susan chooses to invest her time, talent, and leadership.

Exploring and Accessing Your Leadership

We all want to make some kind of difference. I hope that, in reading this book, you have identified with certain aspects of each profiled leader, plus our additional examples of women making outstanding contributions. Some will inspire you more than others, and that's a big part of why I chose the women I did. We are all different, and yet what we have in common is our desire to make a difference, to help create a better workplace, community, or world. Like these women, you just never know how far or wide your influence will reach.

What's your dream or vision? What are your secret thoughts about the difference you want to make, whether local or far-reaching? When you look around your workplace, neighborhood, place of worship or community, what do you see that needs to be done? What improvements have you already made for your family, work team, social network, or neighborhood? There's no magic formula for leadership. It's a process of growth and of vision connecting with action. It's an evolution sometimes spawned by revolution, from raw idea to systematic execution.

Some people will read this book, stick it back on the shelf and grab the next one on their "to read" pile. Others will insert a few sticky notes in the parts they like most, and revisit those sections.

A few readers will choose their favorite leaders, make notes in the margins, highlight the passages that "speak to them," and make some decisions about which unstoppable leaders they want to emulate. For them, this book will be a living document they will revisit. They may even journal to measure progress.

Now that you've finished reading *The Unstoppables – Success Strategies from 12 Top Women Leaders to Supercharge Your Career,* what will you do?

In whatever way you choose to use this book, I hope you'll harness the inspiration you've found to keep you on your path toward a life of significance as you step up to greater levels of leadership. As you know, leadership isn't just for the few; it's for everyone—including you.

Our twelve unstoppable leaders demonstrate that at the core of leadership is an unshakable character based on adherence to their deepest values, a clear, shared vision, a commitment to excellence, a willingness to do the work required, and a deep abiding care and concern for the lives of those they serve and beyond. It is the stuff of which credibility is made—a requisite to a loyal following. May their real-life lessons save you years of struggle as you take their wisdom to heart, helping you solve deeper problems, generate better decisions, communicate more clearly, build stronger teams, and contribute in ways you may never fully realize.

Lastly, may the lessons they learned from their mistakes and less than glorious moments encourage you to stay the course when you are tempted to give up. The most important changes in this world have been accomplished by ordinary people who have kept on going despite extraordinary obstacles. May the words of these *unstoppable* leaders help you *keep on keeping on* as you pursue your pathway to outstanding leadership.

PART THREE

GROUP DISCUSSION
QUESTIONS

CHAPTER 1
CORNERSTONE: CHARACTER

1. What has been your greatest challenge, and how did you handle it? What did your response to the challenge you identified say about your character?

2. If you could re-do your response to your greatest challenge, what would you do differently and why? What impact might that have had on your character?

3. When you think of the best leader you have ever known, how would you describe that person's character and why?

4. This one will take courage on your part to honestly answer. What single aspect of your character would you like to change, strengthen, or improve upon that would have the most powerfully transforming effect on your life and on your relationships at home and at work? What one action can you take right now to begin the process of modifying that one aspect of your character?

CHAPTER 2
BECOME INTERNALLY ALIGNED

1. When you consider your values, which ones are the most important to you and why?

2. What actions do you typically take that demonstrate alignment with your values? What impact does personal alignment have on you?

3. Who do you know who lives in accordance with their espoused values? What impact does alignment with values seem to have on that individual? What impact does it have on your perception of that person?

CHAPTER 3

BOOST YOUR BUOYANCY

1. Think of a time when you bounced back from a setback, challenge, mistake, or failure. What attitude, behavior, or skill helped you to be resilient?

2. What lesson did you learn from this experience that you have carried forward to more effectively address other challenges in your personal life or career?

3. Who is the most resilient person you know? From your perspective, what makes it possible for that individual to consistently bounce back?

CHAPTER 4

BELIEVE IN YOURSELF

1. Now that you have read the chapter on believing in yourself, what one thing could you do to bolster your self-confidence?

2. What combination of qualities or strengths do you possess that make you unique?

3. What have you done, or could you do, to further develop your unique qualities or strengths? What difference might that make to your self-confidence?

CHAPTER 5:
CORNERSTONE: COMMITMENT

1. What parallels can you draw in your life from the Candy Lightner story? What person, vision, cause, or organization are you passionately committed to?

2. How do your actions help support or advance the object of your commitment?

3. Who is the most committed person, almost driven by their passion, you know? What do they do that demonstrates their commitment? What has been the impact of their commitment?

CHAPTER 6
FIND YOUR JAZZ

1. Commitment is born from passion. What do you feel passionate about? What impact has that passion had on your desire and ability to take action?

2. Not everyone has a burning passion for their current job for a variety of reasons. If that is you, how do you find your jazz?

3. Imagine having found your jazz. What difference might that have on your energy, drive, and behavior? What impact might that have on your career, life, and future?

CHAPTER 7
FORGE AHEAD WITH FORTITUDE

1. Identify one area in your life where increased expectations of yourself and others would yield the greatest benefit. How can you internalize and communicate these higher expectations?

2. How might raising the bar on attitudinal and behavioral expectations spark a positive transformation in your area or organization?

3. Who do you know that operates from high expectations of themselves and others? What observable impact have they had in their organization?

CHAPTER 8
FORTIFY YOUR FOUNDATION

1. Pinpoint one attitude, behavior, or skill that you would like to develop to fortify your foundation? In what way would it better serve you and others?

2. What might be holding you back from developing in this area? Is it real or imagined? If real, what can you do to change it?

3. The twelve unstoppable women leaders talked about the importance of mentors. Do you have a mentor? Are you actively seeking your mentor's guidance or support? If you do not have a mentor, where might there be a possibility of a mentor? How would you approach that person?

CHAPTER 9
CORNERSTONE: CORE WORK

1. Based on your personal experience, when you think about the core work required to become an unstoppable leader, what immediately comes to mind?

2. Again, based on your personal experience, what action by a leader you respect or admire has had the greatest positive impact on you? What leadership lessons did you internalize by this example?

3. Assuming you wish to foster the development of your leadership competencies, what activities could you engage in to broaden your skill base? Read more books, take some classes, join a professional association, find a coach, work toward a degree, etc.

CHAPTER 10

CREATE AND EXECUTE A COMPELLING VISION

1. What is your vision? For yourself? For your organization? For your cause? Do you have the courage to make your vision a reality? If faced with a challenge, how can you transform that into fuel for the pursuit of your vision?

2. What difference will the accomplishment of your vision have on you, others, your organization, or larger community?

3. What strategies could you employ to enlist others into your vision? How might you go about sharing your vision?

CHAPTER 11

CRAFT A 3-C TEAM

1. As you think of your role as leader, how does courage impact your ability to lead? In what one small way could you be more courageous? What might be standing in your way of being more courageous right now, and how can you summon it?

2. Our leaders commented on the importance of finding team members who possess complementary strengths. In a leadership role, what strengths would you be looking for to complement your own so you can fill the competency gap?

3. In this chapter we discussed the term holding the rope. Whom do you trust to hold the rope for you and any other team member? Besides being trustworthy, what other qualities do the "rope holders" possess that causes you to select them?

CHAPTER 12

CULTIVATE CRITICAL RELATIONSHIPS

1. Great leaders recognize the importance of good relationships with all kinds of people. When you think about being strategic in forming good relationships, with whom would it be wise to form relationships? What might be the results?

2. When you think about those with whom it would be wise to develop a strong connection, what actions could you take right now to begin creating those connections?

3. Thinking proactively, what actions on your part would promote a higher level of mutual respect and trust within your area of the organization?

CHAPTER 13

CORNERSTONE: CONTRIBUTION

1. When you think of someone who contributed significantly to your life, who comes to mind? What contribution did this person make, and what difference did they make for you?

2. Take a moment to think about ways in which you have contributed to the lives of others. Who comes to mind and how did you make things better for them?

3. What significant contributions do you think about; things you'd like to do for certain individuals or the greater good? How will you go about making these things happen?

CHAPTER 14

LEAD A LIFE OF SERVICE

1. In what ways are you being "of service" to your team? How about your organization as a whole? Your community?

2. If contribution to the larger community hasn't been a focus for you, what personal interests do you have where you could make some measurable contributions?

3. Think of someone who contributes their time and talent to serve their cause or the larger community. How would you describe the differences this person has made?

CHAPTER 15

LEAVE A LASTING LEGACY

1. What lasting legacy would you like to leave? Why?

2. What will you need to do and who will you need to be as a leader to leave this legacy?

3. Identify someone you would like to emulate. What legacy have this person left that has inspired you to pattern yourself after them?

CHAPTER 16
LOOK AFTER WHAT'S ENTRUSTED TO YOU

1. Our twelve unstoppable leaders identified work-life balance as critical to the success of a leader. Describe your current work-life balance and if it is anywhere close to what you want it to be. If not, what would you need to do to gain greater balance?

2. What kind of support system do you have in place? Is it sufficient? If not, what is the negative impact on you and others? If it is balanced, what is the positive impact it has on you and others?

3. When you consider what you have learned from our twelve unstoppable leaders regarding work-life balance and how they make time for their priorities, what ideas for guaranteeing balance make the greatest sense to you?

CHAPTER 17
CONCLUSION: THE LEADER NEXT DOOR

1. If you yearn to make a difference right where you are, where is a good place to start? What can you do to be of greater service in your home, your organization, your community?

2. What is your dream or vision? What are your secret thoughts about the differences you want to make? When you look around you, what needs to be done?

3. What might be standing in your way of moving in the direction of that vision or dream? What step are you willing to take? Who can you ask to help you on your journey?

ENDNOTES

1. Pat Head Summit, with Sally Jenkins. *Sum It Up!*
    New York: Crown Archetype, 1987. Kindle edition.

2. "Her Story" *The Pat Summitt Foundation.* January 4, 2016.
    http://www.patsummitt.org/our_role/pats_story/her_story.aspx

3. Dale Wimbrow, *The Guy in the Glass.* The American Magazine,
    May, 1934.

4. Jim Rohn, *Leading an Inspired Life.* Nightingale-Conant Corporation,
    Niles, Illinois, 1963.

5. Ronald Wilson Reagan, 40th President of the United States.
    Commencement Address. McAlister Field House May 15, 1993.
    http://www3.citadel.edu/pao/addresses/reagan.htm

6. Madeline Levine, PhD. *The Price of Privilege: How Parental
    Pressure and Material Advantage Are Creating a Generation of
    Disconnected and Unhappy Kids.* (New York, NY: Harper Collins
    Publisher, 2008)

7. Stan Linhorst, "Patricia Numann overcame obstacles to become a
    renowned surgeon, leading change worldwide," *CNY Conversations,*
    (10 August 2014) Page D-3 in the Business section of
    The Post-Standard in Syracuse, N.Y.

8. Candy Lightner Biography," *Bio. People,* November 26, 2106.
    http://www.biography.com/people/candy-lightner-21173669

9. "Candy Lightner Facts," *Biography, Your Dictionary,* November 26,
    2015, **http://biography.yourdictionary.com/candy-lightner**

10. "Commitment." *Merriam-Webster .com.* 2015.
    http://www.merriam-webster.com/dictionary/commitment

11. Vince Lombardi, *What It Takes to Be #1: Vince Lombardi on Leader-
    ship.* (McGraw Hill Education, 2003).

12. Marlo Thomas, *The Right Words at the Right Time.* (New York: Atria Books, 2002).

13. Frank O'Dea, *When All You Have is Hope* (Ontario, Canada: Penguin Canada, 2007).

14. Megan Rose Dickey, *"This is Google CEO Larry Page's Grand Vision for Changing the World,"* Business Insider Tech, March 24, 2014, **http://www.businessinsider.com/ google-ceo-larry-page-change-the-world-2014-315**

15. Patricia Caruso, *"Operating a Corrections System in a Depressed Economy: How Michigan Copes,"* EBSCO Host Connections, Corrections Today, February 10, 2010,

16. Michael Krantz/San Francisco and Steve Jobs, "Steve Jobs at 44," Time Magazine, October 10, 1999, **http://content.time.com/time/printout/0,8816,32207,00.html**

17. Max Nisen Max Nisen, *"The most important leadership lesson Microsoft's new CEO learned from Bill Gates,"* Quartz, February 20, 2014. **http://qz.com/179282/leadership-lesson-microsoft-new-ceo-satya-nadella-learned-from-bill-gates**

18. "Complementary." Merriam-Webster.com. **http://www.merriam-webster.com/dictionary/complementary**

19. "Joe E. Martin," *Wikipedia, The Free Encyclopedia,* **https://en.wikipedia.org/wiki/Joe_E._Martin**

20. Matthew 25:14-30 English Standard Version (ESV)

21. Stephanie Marton, "The Mysterious Success of Female-Led Firms," Forbes, February 20, 2013. **http://www.forbes.com/sites/85broads/2013/02/20/ the-mysterious-success-of-female-led-firms/#49d3fde23105**

Mary Jane Mapes

Leadership Strategist and Business Relationship Expert

Mary Jane Mapes, BS, MA, CSP, is the author of three books, including the Amazon bestseller, *You CAN Teach a Pig to Sing – Create Great Relationships...with Anyone, Anytime, Anywhere*, and *The Art of Fielding Questions with Finesse – A Guide to Handling Difficult People, Sensitive Situation, and Tough Questions.* Mary Jane specializes in helping both executive and high potential leaders and entrepreneurs to develop irresistible influence, create deeper levels of trust and commitment, and cultivate more engaged employees. In over 25 years of writing, speaking, coaching, and consulting experience, Mary Jane has helped build powerful teams, create exceptional leaders, and develop and turn around floundering businesses.

As president and CEO of The Aligned Leader Institute, her client list includes leaders and audiences from some of the world's best known corporations and public sector organizations.

Mary Jane is nationally accredited speaker with an uncanny ability to hit the stage, creating an instant connection with her audience. She consistently receives rave reviews for her thought-provoking content, laugh-out-loud humor, and life-changing ideas. Her infectious energy, humor, authenticity, and interaction with her audiences make Mary Jane a rare presenter whose messages are memorable for years to come.

Contact Mary Jane Mapes: **http://maryjanemapes.com**
or **http://alignedleaderinstitute.com**

Follow Mary Jane's leadership blog at:
http://maryjanemapes.com/leadership-development

Check us out at:
http://MyUnstoppableCareer.com

Made in the USA
Charleston, SC
02 June 2016